Tales, 'Trails and Tommyknockers

Stories from Colorado's Past

by
Myriam Friggens

Illustrated by Gene Coulter

Johnson Books, Boulder, Colorado

Copyright 1979 by Myriam Friggens
Library of Congress Catalog Card Number 79-84876
ISBN: 0-933472-01-3

Fourteenth Printing 2002

Printed in the United States
by
Johnson Publishing Company
1880 South 57th Court
Boulder, Colorado 80301

To my father, who sparked my interest in western history.

CONTENTS

PREFACE

Colorado has had an exciting and colorful past. Dinosaurs, Cliff Dwellers, Indians, explorers, trappers, traders, miners, cowboys and settlers have all been part of its story. Even the formation of the land has been fascinating. *Tales, Trails and Tommyknockers* does not attempt to touch upon every significant event that took place in the state. It merely introduces children to some of the romantic lore and legend which have uniquely distinguished Colorado. The stories in the book have been selected more for dramatic narrative appeal than historical significance. However, history has been treated accurately wherever introduced.

It is the author's hope that *Tales, Trails and Tommyknockers* will motivate its young readers and their families to explore more of their exciting and unusual state.

ACKNOWLEDGMENTS

Writing *Tales, Trails and Tommyknockers* has been a richly rewarding experience. I would like to acknowledge several people whose expertise and encouragement have helped make this book a reality: Louisa Ward Arps, noted Colorado historian, for helpful suggestions on research; Kenneth Carpenter, paleontology student at the University of Colorado, for the chapter on dinosaurs; Bob Rothe, local railroad buff, for the chapters on Otto Mears and the Moffat Road; the State Historical Society of Colorado and the Western History Department of the Denver Public Library for illustrations; Joyce Hart and Kitty Leonard, Boulder Valley teachers, for trying out the book in their third grade classes, prior to publication. I am especially grateful to Jerome Brondfield, juvenile author and editor, for critically evaluating the manuscript and encouraging me to publish. The moral support of all these helpful friends has been greatly appreciated. But I am particularly indebted to two people: Gene Coulter, whose sensitive and spirited illustrations bring the book alive, and Barbara Mussil, my publisher.

Cowboys and Castles

It was a cold, gray day in December. Two cowboys were riding along the rim of a high, green mesa in southwest Colorado. They were hunting for cattle that had strayed from their ranch in the Mancos Valley. Tracking the animals had been difficult. After crossing an icy river, the men zigzagged up the steep side of a canyon. Underbrush scraped the legs of their panting horses. Then snow began to fall, making it even harder to follow the cow tracks.

Upon reaching the top, the men reined in their horses and dismounted. While the animals rested, the cowboys walked out to the edge of the windswept mesa. They stood looking over the canyon. One of them kicked loose a rock and sent it tumbling far down into the emptiness below. But they never found out if it hit bottom. For suddenly, with a gasp of amazement, one of the cowboys grasped his partner's arm. He pointed across the canyon. Opposite them, about half a mile away, was a great cave in the side of a cliff. Tucked under the overhanging rock, they saw a shining city of stone!

The little flat-roofed houses were crowded together like the many rooms in a castle. Some were even perched crazily on top of one another. A round tower, three stories high, stood near the center. The cowboys blinked their eyes and shook the snow from their faces. Were they imagining things? No! The castle was really there in the cliff! Dark window and door openings stared out of the deserted buildings like tiny eyes watching them from afar.

The stray cattle were forgotten. Using their lariats, the cowboys tied several tree limbs together to make a ladder. Then they let themselves down over the edge of the dangerous cliff. At last they reached the bottom. Scrambling up through the juniper and pinon trees, they stepped into the ghostly ruins. Their voices echoed spookily across the empty rooms. Who were the mysterious people who had once lived here? And why had they disappeared?

The men found a stone ax in the dust. Its blade was still attached to the wooden handle. Excitedly, they began digging around. Soon they unearthed pottery

Mysterious Cliff Palace, the "castle" accidentally discovered by
the Wetherill brothers while they were out tracking lost cattle.

bowls, mugs and large water jars. The pottery had
beautiful black and white designs on it. It seemed almost as if the owners must be nearby, and might appear at any moment. But the crumbling brick walls
and caved-in roofs of the houses were proof that no one
had lived here for hundreds of years.

The cowboys stumbled over three skeletons partly
buried in the rubble. Suddenly, one of the men had an
upsetting thought. Could this be the place that his Ute
Indian friend, Acowitz, had once warned him about?
"I will tell you a secret—a thing unknown to white
men," he had said. "Deep in a canyon, high, high, in
the rocks, the biggest house of the old people lies

Spruce Tree House, Mesa Verde

hidden. Utes never go there because it is a sacred place. The spirits of the dead must not be disturbed—or we, too, shall die.''

There was something about this spooky place that made the cowboys' blood run cold. Shuddering, they left the skeletons and pottery exactly as they had found them and quickly departed. The wind was beginning to blow the snow harder now. Their dusty footprints soon disappeared under a blanket of white, leaving behind no trace of their visit.

* * * *

The cowboys' names were Richard Wetherill and Charlie Mason. The date was December 18, 1888. The castle in the side of the cliff was, of course, Cliff Palace—largest of the now famous Mesa Verde Cliff Dwellings. Wetherill and Mason were the first white men to enter the silent ruin, and they gave it its name. Contrary to the Indians' warning, the cowboys did not die after discovering the ruin. They went on to discover

Cliff Palace, Mesa Verde   State of Colorado

many more cliff dwellings in Mesa Verde. Richard
Wetherill also explored ancient ruins in New Mexico,
Arizona and Utah. Most of the treasures he found were
long ago placed in museums.

America's "first apartment houses" have now become a national park. Today there are dozens of cliff
dwellings you can visit. Guides take you through the
deserted ruins, where you can climb ladders and peer
through the tiny doors. You can even step down into
the kivas (big, underground rooms) where the men
held secret ceremonies. In the museum are many interesting exhibits showing how the people lived a
thousand years ago.

Scientists now think that they left their cliff houses
after many, many years without rain. Without water,
their corn and beans died, and they had nothing to eat.
They may have traveled to new lands in the Southwest.
But we are not sure. The story of the Cliff Dwellers is
still as mysterious as the day the cowboys first discovered their exciting castles.

Prunes:
The
Prospector's Partner

If you've ever spent the night on a farm, you've probably been awakened by a crowing rooster. But if you had lived in an early day mining camp in Colorado, the braying of a "Rocky Mountain Canary" might have roused you. The Rocky Mountain Canary was not a songbird, however. It was a burro! The miners jokingly called these shaggy little animals "canaries," because of their loud and unmusical "hee-haw."

But without the faithful, hard-working burro, Colorado's history would have been very different. There would have been no early gold or silver mining. For how would the rich ore have been found, dug out or hauled to market? Cars and trucks were unheard of, and the little narrow-gauge trains would not come along until years later.

Prunes, Colorado's most famous burro, celebrating his fortieth birthday with some hardrock miners from the Fairplay-Alma area.

The burro carried all the food, supplies and equipment to the far away mining camps. He picked his way carefully over steep and winding trails. Even the heavy timbers used to build the mine shafts had to be carried on his back. And before the little ore cars could roll, the burro, of course, had to haul in the rails.

In the Fairplay-Alma area in South Park there once lived a very famous burro. He was called Prunes because his dark, rough coat was about the color of that dried fruit. He was owned by a prospector named Rupe Sherwood. Rupe was always out looking for gold. Poor overloaded Prunes carried Rupe's blanket, gold pan, frying pan, coffee pot, ax, pick, shovel, rope, flour, bacon, coffee and sugar. He also carried oats for himself.

While Rupe was panning for gold in the mountain streams, Prunes was free to graze. But whenever Rupe hunted for gold in the canyons so he could stake out a claim, Prunes worked hard. Rupe would harness the burro to his pick which he used like a plow. Prunes would pull the pick back and forth, loosening the soil and rocks that might contain ore. He also dragged away the big boulders that were too heavy to lift. Then Rupe would dig up a blanketful of dirt, loading it onto a sled. Prunes pulled it down to the stream, where Rupe could wash out the gold.

But panning was hard work. So Rupe began making what the prospectors called "Long Toms" and sluice boxes. A "Long Tom" was a hollowed out log which he rocked back and forth like a cradle. A screen at the bottom caught the gold, after the water and gravel had sloshed out. In the sluice box, Rupe washed dirt and gravel down a long trough with steps in it. These steps, called "riffles," held the heavier gold while the gravel and water rushed on through. Rupe then poured mercury on the finer ore so that the gold would roll up into a tiny ball. Prunes hauled the lumber to make these sluices and Long Toms.

Colorado Historical Society

Rupe preferred placer mining for himself along the stream beds. He didn't like working in the mines. But he wasn't always lucky enough to find his own gold. So sometimes he and Prunes would have to work at hardrock mining for somebody else. That was how Prunes became so famous. At one time or another, he worked all the mines in the Fairplay-Alma district. While Rupe dug out the ore underground, Prunes helped haul it up. He let himself be hitched to a wheel which lifted a loaded bucket by means of a steel cable. Of course he had to walk to turn the wheel.

After the ore reached the top, Prunes joined the burro packtrain which carried it down to the mill. The hardworking little animals would trudge along single file, bulging ore sacks hanging from their sides. At the mill, big round stones rubbing together crushed the gold out of the rocks.

Prospector and his best friend set out for the gold panning country.

Rupe and Prunes were partners for almost fifty years. Rupe never did get rich, but his diggings brought him enough money to retire in comfort. During the icy winters he would rent out his Fairplay cabin and move to Denver. The townspeople lovingly looked after Prunes, feeding him hay, biscuits and pancakes. When Rupe returned in May, Prunes would "hee-haw" a hearty welcome.

On Rupe's eightieth birthday his friends held a big party. Prunes celebrated with a bag of oats. But he had great difficulty eating because he no longer had any teeth. That winter, after Rupe returned to Denver, a blinding blizzard struck Fairplay. Prunes sought shelter in an old, tumbledown shed. But the wind blew the door shut, trapping him inside. When the children finally found him he was very weak and ill. The mothers fed him stacks of pancakes, and he managed to hang on until Rupe returned in the spring. But the 63-year-old burro was barely alive. The towns-people decided that the kindest thing to do was to shoot Prunes. Sorrowfully, Rupe agreed.

The people of Fairplay and Alma missed Prunes terribly. And they decided to do something about it. They collected money to build a monument to their faithful friend. When it was finished, they moved his bones to a nearby grave. Then they held a ceremony. Rupe read "Me and Prunes"—a poem he had written for the occasion. But with his old pal gone, life was empty for Rupe. A year later he became seriously ill himself. Before dying, he asked to have his body cremated and the ashes buried beside his burro. Rupe's wish was granted.

Today, on a street in Fairplay, you can see this monu-ment to a miner's best friend. It is simple: just a few words carved on a stone slab, beneath a bronze picture of Prunes. Here the remains of Rupe and Prunes appear to rest peacefully forever. But who knows? Perhaps these lifelong partners are out tramping the heavenly hills to-gether, still prospecting for gold!

Located prominently on the main street of Fairplay is the town's memorial to Prunes, its most celebrated resident.

Colorado Historical Society

Silver Heels
in the Sky

A few miles from Fairplay is a ghost town called Buckskin Joe. It was named for Joseph Higginbottom, an old prospector who always wore tanned deerskin clothes. According to the story, a beautiful dancer came to the Buckskin Joe mining area in the 1860's. We are not absolutely certain that she lived in Buckskin Joe, however. Fairplay and Alma also claim her as their heroine. To tell the truth, we are not even certain that she lived at all. But the old timers used to swear that she did. They even pointed out her cabin which they said was still standing among the trees . . .

She was not a great or important lady. She was just a dance hall girl who entertained the weary, fun-starved miners. She had many dancing partners. As she danced, gracefully moving feet flashed in the lamplight. They called her Silver Heels because she wore silver slippers which matched the ribbon in her dark brown hair.

Silver Heels had a boyfriend named Bill. One winter evening he became very ill with a disease called smallpox. Doctors and hospitals were few in the mining camps of those days. People had not yet learned about taking shots, and medicines were not as powerful as they are today. Silver Heels tried her best to nurse Bill, but after a few hours the miner died in her arms.

The dreaded disease spread like wildfire. Almost overnight everyone in the entire camp was dangerously ill. Saloons, dance halls and gambling houses were closed, and many of the mines shut down. Each day more people were buried under the snow in the little cemetery on the hill. A telegram was sent to Denver asking for nurses. But only two or three came. Few women were willing to risk their lives or even their looks by going among the dying miners, for smallpox is a highly contagious disease which leaves its victims pockmarked for life.

But Silver Heels was not afraid. Throughout the long, dark winter she went from cabin to cabin, caring for the sick and comforting the dying. She cooked, washed and cleaned as well. Then one day she became ill herself. The surviving townspeople nursed her tenderly for many weeks. At last she was well. By this time spring had returned, bringing the warm, healing sunshine. Little by little the town recovered, and the mines and businesses were reopened. The terrible sickness had passed.

Then one day somebody remembered Silver Heels. The miners decided that something should be done to reward her. They collected $5,000 and took the money to her cabin. But no one answered their knocking. Silver Heels had disappeared. The townspeople searched for her everywhere. But they finally had to give up in despair. The money was returned to the miners.

Colorado Historical Society

Early day Fairplay. Its main street resembles the nearby nineteenth century ''ghost town'' museum of South Park City.

Years later, a woman wearing a heavy black veil was seen in the cemetery, weeping over the graves. When anyone approached, she would quickly vanish into the trees. Although no one ever saw her face, the miners felt certain it was Silver Heels, come back to mourn her dead comrades. She wore the veil because her once beautiful face was now scarred and ugly. Smallpox had stolen her outward beauty. But to the grateful people of Buckskin Joe, her inner beauty would live forever. They named a lovely mountain in her honor! Mt. Silver Heels towers above Fairplay, its snow-clad summit shimmering in the moonlight—like the dancing silver in a brave girl's heels!

* * * *

Colorado has dozens of ghost towns like Buckskin Joe and Fairplay. Each has its story. Wouldn't it be fun to step into a time machine, set the dials back 100 years, and find yourself in a rip-roaring Colorado mining camp? This is impossible, of course. But you can do the next best thing: visit South Park City, at the edge of Fairplay. South Park

City is not a ghost town, since it never was a real town. It is a large, outdoor museum, showing what life was like in a mining camp between 1870 and 1900. There are more than twenty-five buildings, a railroad station, stagecoach inn, stagecoach, covered wagon and even a narrow-gauge engine. Although the buildings have been fixed up for the museum, most of them really did come from ghost towns in the area. A few of them even stand right where they were built.

You can see an old mine shaft from Buckskin Joe, and an arrastra (uh-ras-truh) from Buckskin Joe Creek. An arrastra was a huge, round stone, scooped out like a basin. A smaller stone, placed inside it, was fastened to a wheel. The miner, or his mule, would walk around the arrastra turning the wheel and dragging the heavy stone behind him. This was one of the earliest ways to grind gold ore out of the rock.

In the mining museum you can learn much about placer mining equipment and methods. The stores, houses and offices are full of interesting things people used in olden times. And don't forget to pay a visit to the schoolhouse! You can almost hear the children reciting their ABC's as they bend over their little gray slates!

Wild Horses in the Sand

On moonlit nights, so it is said, you can sometimes see them—huge, web-footed horses racing over the sand, manes and tails flying. They glide by as silently and gracefully as a dream. But no cowboy has ever caught one. They are faster than the wind. These are the wild horses that, according to legend, travel over the Great Sand Dunes of Colorado.

Is the story really true? Well, perhaps partly. Of course nobody believes in web-footed horses. But bands of wild horses with unusually broad hooves *do* roam the edges of the dunes. Back in the 1500s, the Spaniards brought the

Light plays across the swirling, ever shifting sands of the Great Sand Dunes National Monument in southern Colorado.

first horses to Colorado. The early day Utes spoke of "men with much hair on their faces, wearing iron shirts, and riding wild, snorting animals." Perhaps these moonlit mustangs are descended from those early "snorting animals." They could have developed broad, fan-shaped hooves from 400 years of running over the dunes. Or maybe it's just that the wind sometimes blows the ever shifting sands into horselike shapes.

Anyway, the biggest and highest sand dunes in America are in the San Luis Valley of southern Colorado. They are surrounded on three sides by snowcapped mountains. To the north and east lie the Sangre de Cristo ("Blood of Christ") mountains, and on the west tower the San Juans. The smaller San Juan hills rise on the south.

Here is how this giant sand pile is formed. Mountain streams carry sand, silt and gravel down to the San Luis Valley. Because there is little rain, few plants grow on the valley floor. There is nothing to stop the blowing sand until it piles up against the mountains. At the bottom of the high peaks it is trapped in a great mound 1500 feet deep. A whole city could be buried in it!

The colors of the Great Sand Dunes change constantly with the light. They are like huge mounds of magic ice cream—now vanilla, now chocolate, now maplenut. The setting sun turns them strawberry red or purple. When the wind is blowing freely over the sliding sands, you can sometimes hear eerie voices! That is probably why the Indians called them "singing sands." They must have visited them often because many arrowheads and Indian skeletons have been found in the dunes.

After the Spanish explorers, the next white men to see the Dunes were members of Lieutenant Zebulon Pike's famous expedition. In 1806, the United States government sent Pike out west to search for the beginnings of the Red River. At that time southern Colorado belonged to Spain. It was important to find this river because we believed it to be the boundary between Spanish and U.S. territory. (Later on, the Arkansas River became the true boundary.)

After crossing the Sangre de Cristo Mountains, Pike and his men rode down into the San Luis Valley. Here they discovered a "sea of sand." Climbing one of the highest dunes, Pike saw a shining river in the distance through his spyglass. But it was not the Red River, as Pike thought. It was the mighty Rio Grande. Soon after, Pike was captured by Spanish soldiers when he raised the U.S. flag beside the Conejos fork of this river. They took him to Chihuahua (Chee wa wa), but he was allowed to return home before long.

There are many fascinating tales about the dunes. Prospectors and even shepherds with whole flocks have supposedly wandered into the sands, never to be seen again. A creek flows along the edge of the dunes for several miles. Then it suddenly disappears into the ground. After crossing the mountains, a wagon train once

28

camped beside Medano (Sandy) Creek. The mules were turned out to graze, and drivers slipped into their bedrolls for the night. The next morning, wagon train, drivers, and mules all had mysteriously vanished. Had the creek flooded during the night, swallowing them up? Or had they perhaps been sucked under by flowing sand? No one will ever know. The whispering Dunes guard their secrets well.

* * * *

If you visit the Great Sand Dunes today you won't have to worry about disappearing! People climb all over the dunes, sinking in usually no farther than their ankles. Sliding down these huge hills of sand is great fun on a sunny day. Some people even like to walk on the dunes in the rain, when the sand is firmer.

There is more than just sand at the Great Sand Dunes National Monument, however. Mountains are all around you. You can take hikes and nature walks, see the exhibits in the Visitor's Center, or just relax in the campgrounds. But don't expect to see any wild horses—they are only a legend!

Robbers on Raton Pass

The night was dark and gloomy. Thick clouds blotted out the stars, and just a thin sliver of moonlight glimmered through the trees. Uncle Dick Wootton, a bearded old mountain man, let the fire die down to a pile of ashes. Surely at this late hour no stagecoach passengers would be stopping at his roadhouse. He gulped down one last slug

"Uncle Dick" Wootton, in trapper's outfit. The tiny town of Wootton below Raton Pass was named for this Colorado mountain man.

of his favorite "firewater," Taos Lightning. Then he turned down his kerosene lamp, placed a couple of pistols under his pillow, and climbed into bed.

He didn't go to sleep right away, though. He lay there in the stillness thinking about the money his successful toll road and stage stop were bringing him. It was one of the first such roads in Colorado—and building it had not been easy. First, he had to get permission from the people of two territories because the road would pass through both New Mexico and Colorado. (At this time Colorado was not yet a state). Then he had to hire men to cut through mountains, blast out rocks, and build log bridges.

The road followed an old Indian trail over Raton Pass, which Wootton knew well. In 1858 he had driven a whole wagon train of supplies across these mountains where only horses had passed before. But because he had to chop his way through a forest, it took him nearly a month to travel fifty miles.

So in 1865, he decided to build a road. His dirt trail soon became a very busy highway. Besides stagecoaches carrying passengers and mail, there were freighters with wagonloads of trade goods bound for New Mexico. Army troops also marched over the pass, as did Mexicans and Indians.

Now a fellow doesn't go to all the trouble and expense of building a public road for nothing. He intends to collect money from the people passing over it. How else would the road pay for itself? Most of Wootton's travelers understood this, paid up promptly, and continued through the gate. But now and then someone would come along who didn't want to pay. A gun pointed in the troublemaker's face usually changed his mind, however. Indians, of course, were allowed to pass free, as were officers of the law. These deputies were usually after horse and cattle thieves, heading with their stolen animals over the pass into New Mexico.

Uncle Dick chuckled to himself in the darkness. Yes, running a stagestop hotel and toll road had been anything but dull. He had certainly met up with all kinds of people. But tonight everything was quiet. He rolled over and closed his eyes.

Suddenly a scuffling noise outside made him sit up, wide-awake. He heard a muffled thud, followed by the tinkle of broken glass. Was somebody trying to break in? Jumping out of bed, he sprang to the window, Four men, their arms loaded with whiskey bottles, were sneaking out of the bar next door. The Ross gang! And they were headed his way! Uncle Dick grabbed his rifle. Poking the muzzle through a broken pane of glass, he waited quietly. When the robbers were within ten feet of the window, he shoved the gleaming muzzle out a little farther. "Halt!" he shouted, "or I'll shoot!"

The robbers stopped short in surprise. Then Jack Ross, leader of the gang, spoke up: "Sorry to disturb your sleep, pardner," he drawled, "but it does get mighty cold and lonesome around these here parts at night. Me and my buddies have got a long way to ride. We would sure like to bed down for the night. Now how about showin' a little hospitality and gettin' up to let us in?"

"Sorry, boys, but you're out of luck," snapped Uncle Dick. "I know who you are and what you're up to. And I have no intention of opening my house to a gang of robbers at this hour of the night. Now I'm giving you just thirty seconds to put that liquor back where you found it and clear out of here—or I'll blow your brains out! How's *that* for hospitality?"

"Uncle Dick's" house (now much enlarged) on the old toll road site.

The Ross gang didn't take time to reply. They grabbed their horses and were gone like a flash. Just then Uncle Dick heard the midnight stage come rattling down the mountain. So that had been the bandits' plan! Hold up old Uncle Dick before meeting the stage! Well, they wouldn't get by with it so easily. When the horses pulled in at Uncle Dick's there were eight passengers aboard. Wootton warned them about the "road agents" up ahead, and loaned them a few extra pistols. Then the driver started on towards Trinidad. But the stagecoach never met up with the robbers. Perhaps the Ross gang had had enough of Uncle Dick Wootton's trigger-happy hospitality!

* * * *

Uncle Dick Wootton's toll road adventures were only a small part of a long and exciting life. As a youth, he trapped beaver with the mountain men, and fought in the war against Mexico. Later, he captured wild buffalo calves and raised them on his farm near Pueblo. During the Pikes Peak Gold Rush, Wootton opened the first saloon and general store in Denver. When the railroads came in 1878, he sold his toll road to the Santa Fe line and retired.

But Colorado has not forgotten Uncle Dick. The little "town" of Wootton now stands below Raton Pass, just north of the Colorado state line. It is on the site of the old toll gate. You can see the sign from highway I-25 as you cruise along over the Interstate—on what was once just an Indian trail!

A
Famous
Peak
and a Song

The Great Spirit was restless. He sat alone up in the empty sky, with nothing to look at and no one to talk to. He needed something to do. So he decided to make a mountain. He took a large stone and began turning it around and around. Soon he had gouged out a big hole in the sky. He poured ice and snow down through the hole. It piled up higher and higher, forming itself into a great peak.

The Great Spirit stepped from the clouds to the top of the peak. He put His fingers into the ground. Trees and plants sprang up everywhere. The melting snow began to dribble down over the sides of the mountain. So He scraped out channels with His staff, making rivers. With His mighty breath He blew on the leaves, turning them into birds. He waved His staff in the air, and many other animals appeared. The grizzly, who stood on two legs, He made master of them all.

Then one day a terrible thing happened. The Daughter of the Great Spirit wandered too far from home. She came down to the mountain, where she fell under the power of the grizzly. He forced her to marry him, and they had many, many children. The Great Spirit protected all of these children, whom he called "Indians." But He was still very angry with the grizzly for marrying His daughter. So He punished the grizzly and all other bears, by making them walk on four legs from that day forth.

The Ute Indians believed that this was how the world—with Pikes Peak in the center—was created. Native people didn't learn about nature in school, as we do, so of course they didn't believe in science. They had their own stories about the beginnings of things which we call myths.

How do scientists think that this great mountain was formed? Geologists (people who study the earth) tell us that the famous mountain is about one billion years old. In the beginning there was no mountain. There was only a huge mass of hot, flowing liquid deep down in the earth. On top of this liquid rock was the solid crust of the earth.

Pikes Peak, whose "Purple Mountain Majesty" inspired Katherine Lee Bates to write the poem, "America the Beautiful."

Lieutenant Zebulon Montgomery Pike who came west in 1806 to explore what is now Colorado. Although he never found the river boundary between the United States and Spanish territory, he did discover the now famous "Pikes Peak."

Now the liquid never did come up through the crust and explode like a volcano. Colorado does have mountains that were formed in this way. But Pikes Peak is not one of them.

The flowing liquid that was to become Pikes Peak simply cooled slowly. At the same time, the older rock above it began to wear away. This took millions of years. But finally the upper crust wore away completely. Pikes Peak, which had by now cooled and formed into granite, was left on top. Then the Ice Age came along, covering the peak with glaciers. These huge, moving ice fields carved lakes, steep sides, and sharp ridges on the mountain. (Much as you'd carve a face on a bar of soap). And that is how the two-and-a-half-mile-high mountain came to be.

But how did the 14,110-foot peak get its name? Zebulon Montgomery Pike was an army man. In 1806 the United States government sent him out west to explore part of what is now Colorado. Our country did not look like it does today. Towns and cities were built only on the eastern side of the Mississippi. West of the great river lay wide open Indian country. Spain owned a large chunk of this unexplored territory. But we weren't sure where the exact boundary lines between our two countries were. So Pike was sent west to find them.

He was not very successful in finding the boundary. But he did discover the beginnings of the South Platte and Arkansas Rivers. And he found the peak! His men were marching west along the Arkansas River (near present day Las Animas) when they spotted a mountain in the distance. It looked like a "small blue cloud." Since they were trying to find the beginning of the Red River, Pike decided to climb it for the view. They marched as hard as they could for several days. But the mountain seemed to get no

Colorado Historical Society

Old Manitou and Pikes Peak cog wheel train.

closer! Finally, at the end of twelve days, Pike had to give up. "Highest Peak," he declared, would never be climbed. It was now late November, and snow covered the ground. In freezing, below zero temperatures Pike's soldiers wore only cotton overalls and no stockings! (Later they made moccasins from the hides of buffalo which they shot.)

Pike and his men nearly starved to death during this expedition. Two men even lost their toes through freezing. So it is not surprising that they didn't get around to climbing the mountain! Fourteen years later, however, someone did. Dr. Edwin James was a botanist (person who studies plants) and historian. He climbed the peak in 1820, while he was a member of the Long expedition. (See "A Lady Climbs A Mountain"). Major Long wanted to name it James Peak, in the botanist's honor. But trappers and hunters continued to call it Pikes Peak. So Pikes Peak it became—although Pike did not name it for himself. (Later, a lower peak was named for Dr. James.)

The peak has been a famous landmark for more than 150 years. In 1859, gold seekers with "Pikes Peak or Bust" lettered on their wagons, followed it westward. People from the east, in fact, thought of the whole Rocky Mountain region as "Pikes Peak Country." (It is not Colorado's highest mountain, but it stands out because there

Gold seekers heading for the Pikes Peak country.

are no other high peaks around it. Colorado actually has fifty-three peaks over 14,000 feet high. We call these peaks "The Fourteeners." Mt. Elbert is our state's highest mountain, at 14,431 feet.)

More people have reached the top of Pikes Peak than any other high mountain in the world, except for Japan's Fujiyama. They have gone up by foot, burro, carriage, cog train and car. Every year on Labor Day there is an automobile race to the summit. And on New Year's Eve the Adaman Club climbs the peak and sets off firecrackers on top.

But how many of the peak's visitors have realized that a famous song was born on this mountain? In 1893, a teacher named Katherine Lee Bates was vacationing in Colorado. One day she rode in a carriage to the top of Pikes Peak. She stood gazing out at the magnificent view. Mountain ranges rose all around her. Far out on the plains golden wheat fields waved in the sun. Purple shadows crept slowly over the peak.

Suddenly she exclaimed aloud: "Oh, beautiful! Such spacious skies! Such amber waves of grain!" Do you know what song has these words? You should! It is one of our best loved national anthems. The music was added later. But it was the view from Pikes Peak that inspired Miss Bates to write the poem, "America The Beautiful"!

Baby Doe
Holds On to the
Matchless Mine

It is a winter day in Leadville. Snow falls over the city, gently blurring the outlines of rooftops and chimneys. An old woman trudges along through the waist-deep drifts, up Fryer Hill. Her threadbare, black coat is covered with snow. Beneath it she has wrapped several layers of news-papers about her body. They are tied carefully with string. Gunny sacks cover her feet, and on her head is a man's old cap. Leadville's air, at over 10,000 feet, is thin. She pauses to catch her breath in the high, frosty atmosphere. Then she wraps her woolen muffler more tightly about her neck. Thrusting her stiff, bare hands into her pockets, she pushes on.

At the top of the hill she comes to a weather-beaten old cabin. Behind it stands a deserted mineshaft. The cabin was once a miner's toolhouse, but now she lives alone in it. Wood is piled high beside the entrance. She gathers up an armload and then shuffles inside. The tiny one room shack is cluttered with papers and trash. On the walls are ferns and dried up evergreen boughs. The floor is littered with cardboard boxes and pieces of wood. In one corner stands an unmade bed, covered with a ragged blanket.

The old lady builds a fire in her potbellied stove. Then she sits down to a cold dinner of sowbelly (salt pork) and beans. While she is eating there is a loud knock at the door. Startled, she grabs her shotgun. She peers through her grimy, cobweb covered front window. Then she lays aside her shotgun and opens the door. A neighbor greets her with some fresh deer meat. She takes the meat, thanks him, and quickly disappears inside.

Darkness closes in upon Fryer Hill. Savage winds howl down over the valley. The little cabin creaks and groans as the icy blasts come whistling through its cracks. Inside, the shivering old woman stokes up the fire. Then she settles into her rocking chair with her ouija (we-juh) board. Perhaps tonight she will hear from her dead daughter, Silver Dollar, in the spirit world. The board has letters and numbers on it. She places a small, three-legged table on its surface. Then she rests her fingertips lightly upon the table. She waits for it to "move" and spell out a message.

But no one will ever know if she received one that night. Several days later her body—frozen stiff—is found upon the floor. Her arms are outstretched and her fists clenched. A search is made of the cabin, but there is pitifully little of value. A well worn coin purse, found near her bedside, holds two dollars and a few pennies. On the shelves are some canned foods. That is all.

But stored away somewhere are trunks full of expensive dresses—once belonging to the dead woman. Priceless jewels, painstakingly braided into balls of yarn, lie hidden for safe keeping. For this ragged old woman found dead in a miner's toolshed was not always poor. Once upon a time she was young, rich and beautiful. Her name was Elizabeth McCourt Doe Tabor—but they called her "Baby Doe." In 1883 she became the second wife of H.A.W. Tabor, Leadville's famous "Silver King."

Horace Tabor had owned a grocery store in Leadville. He became a wealthy mine owner quite by accident. One day he "grubstaked" two poor miners. They just happened to strike a very rich lode. And because Tabor had given them food and supplies, they gave him a one-third share in the mine. His good luck continued, and he bought other mines. Before long he became so rich that he couldn't even count all his money. He wore shirts that cost $1,000!

He and Baby Doe were married in Washington, D.C. A president of the United States came to their wedding, where he drank a toast to the young bride's beauty. (She had long, reddish gold hair and blue eyes.) Her gown, which cost $7,000, was trimmed with pearls. She even wore a $75,000 diamond necklace which, people said,

Blue-eyed, golden-haired "Baby Doe"
at the height of her beauty in 1883 when
she married rich Horace Tabor.

had once belonged to Queen Isabella of Spain. (It was Queen Isabella and King Ferdinand who sent Columbus around the world. The necklace worn by Baby Doe was probably pawned back in 1492 to help pay for the voyage.)

After the wedding the Tabors moved into a large mansion in Denver. For the next ten years, while Tabor's silver mines poured forth millions, Baby Doe lived the life of a queen. Servants waited on her hand and foot. She even owned three handsome, horse drawn carriages. When she rode through the streets of Denver she was attended, like Cinderella, by coachmen in fancy uniforms. She wore silks and satins, drank champagne and ate caviar (a very expensive kind of black fish eggs). And she thought her fairytale life would go on forever.

But all too soon it came to an end. For in 1893 the United States government stopped buying silver to use in banking. Gold continued to be valuable. But the price of silver dropped quickly. This brought very bad times to the western states. Silver mines shut down, and thousands of men were thrown out of work. And because miners no longer had money to buy things, stores and businesses also went broke. Many families were without food or shelter. Banks even lost all their money and had to close. Horace Tabor's silver mines became worthless. He and Baby Doe were so penniless that they were forced for awhile to beg from friends. Finally, the city of Denver gave Mr. Tabor the job of postmaster. (He had once spent part of his fortune building a beautiful opera house there).

In 1899 he died, still believing that the price of silver would some day rise again. His favorite Leadville mine was the Matchless. It had once earned him over $2,000 a day. "Promise me," he told Baby Doe as he lay dying,

"Baby Doe" Tabor at Matchless Mine, Lead-ville. Photo taken October 1933, a year or two before she died, alone and penniless.

"promise me that no matter what happens you'll always hold on to the Matchless Mine. There's a treasure in the Matchless. Someday it will again make you millions." It never did. But for the next thirty-six years Baby Doe kept her promise. She guarded the Matchless faithfully. Her frozen body was found in the mine's toolhouse, one bitter March day in 1935. (People think that she probably died of a heart attack, later stiffening in the cold. She was about 81 years old.)

Baby Doe's old cabin still stands beside the Matchless Mine on Fryer Hill. But it has now been cleaned up and made into a small museum. Hundreds of tourists visit it every summer. And perhaps, were she alive, Colorado's former Silver Queen would approve. For she'd always wanted to be famous. And now she is—the world over!

Western History Department,
Denver Public Library

Young "Baby Doe"
wearing one
of her elegant
new gowns.

Bent Blows Up the Fort

Did you know that Colorado once had a castle made of mud and straw? But no kings or queens lived in it. There weren't even any good fairies or wicked witches. The castle did have watchtowers and cannons, though. Soldiers guarded it day and night. And yet this strange fortress was never attacked! Perhaps that is because it was so well protected.

They called it Bent's Old Fort. It was the biggest and most important trading post in what is now southeastern Colorado. The Bent brothers and a Frenchman named Ceran St. Vrain built it during the fur trapping days of the 1830s. Their mud fortress had to be big and strong. It sat out on the eastern plains in the heart of the Indian country. To this famous old fort came the buckskinned mountain men with their beaver pelts. Plains Indians traded buffalo hides for knives, guns, looking glasses and other goods of the white men. During the trading season Cheyenne tipis dotted the countryside around the fort. Guards with loaded rifles walked back and forth along the rooftop.

The inner patio was the busiest, most colorful part of the fort. Indian women strolled about in beaded moccasins and long, deerskin dresses. Traders and bearded mountain men smoked and talked together in the shady plaza. Above the clang of the blacksmith's hammer you could hear horses neighing, mules braying, children crying and men quarreling. The smells of freshly baked bread and roasting buffalo meat hung in the air.

In the 1840s there were no towns or cities in what is now Colorado. The goods traded to the Indians or trappers had to be brought from afar. Starting from Missouri, wagon trains followed the 800-mile long Santa Fe Trail west across the plains to New Mexico. Bent's Fort was their main stopping place along the way. It became the great "shopping center" of the prairies. From St. Louis came shiny beads, calico, hardware and ammunition for rifles. Caravans returning from the Santa Fe end of the trail carried horses, handwoven Navajo blankets and Mexican

Bent's new fort, reconstructed on the banks of the Arkansas River near La Junta, Colorado, at a cost of over two million dollars.

silver dollars. Buffalo robes were sent east to be made into coats, bedding and rugs. And beaver furs ended up on the heads of rich gentlemen in London and Paris who wore tall beaver hats.

Trading went on at the fort for many years. Then in 1846 the United States went to war with Mexico over who should own what we now call Texas. Suddenly, everything changed. American soldiers swarmed over the plains, cutting down cottonwood trees for fuel. The wagon trains almost stopped, and trade slowed to a trickle.

The war was soon over. But then hordes of settlers started coming west. Watering places were muddied and buffalo herds shot down or frightened away. The Indians, who depended upon the big, shaggy animals for food, clothing and shelter, went on the warpath. New Mexico (which had been part of Mexico) made trouble also. The

Spanish people there were bitter about losing the war. They hated having to become American citizens. Charles Bent was named their new governor. But soon after he was murdered in Taos.

All this was horrible enough. But then the final blow came to Bent's Fort. Gold seekers coming across the plains brought with them a terrible disease called cholera (kawl-er-uh). "The Big Cramps," as the Indians called it, spread like wildfire through the tribes. Half of the southern Cheyennes died. Trade at the fort came to a standstill.

The year was 1849. William Bent and Ceran St. Vrain realized that their twenty-year partnership was over. Inside the fort's adobe walls they sipped one last mint julep drink together. Then they shook hands. Ceran mounted his horse and headed east for Missouri. Sadly, William watched him ride off down the trail and disappear into the distance. Then he turned and walked back slowly through the heavy wooden gates.

His footsteps echoed eerily across the deserted courtyard. The sunny patio seemed filled with ghosts from the past: Indians in their beaded buckskins; long-haired, fur-laden trappers; wagon drivers and army men in uniforms. Where were they now?

William sat down and put his head in his hands. His three brothers were all dead. The fort belonged to him. But what would he do with it? Sell it to the United States government? He knew they wanted the old mud fortress for an army post. But they refused to pay him what he felt it was worth. William did not intend to let unfriendly Indians move into it either. They would only use its sheltering walls as a base from which to attack the white man.

No. The last of the Bent brothers decided there was only one thing to do. He ordered his servants to remove every-

William Bent during
Mexican War period.

thing valuable from the rooms. Then he piled the goods onto wagons. He had oxen haul them to a camp five miles down the Arkansas River. His Indian wife, Yellow Woman, followed along on horseback with their children.

Now William was all alone. He rolled kegs of gunpowder into the storage and trading rooms of the fort. Then he lighted a torch. Moving from apartment to apartment, he set fire to the wooden roof beams and leftover piles of junk. He closed the front gate and locked it. Then he rode away. As the flames reached the powder, an earsplitting BOOM-BOOM jarred the prairie. But William Bent did not turn around. He did not even glance back. His trading days at the fort were over.

* * * *

The old fort which William Bent blew up is gone. But today you can visit one just like it! The new Bent's Fort took more than a year to build and cost over two million dollars. It stands right where the old one stood, on the banks of the Arkansas River, near the town of La Junta. It also is made of fireproof adobe (mud mixed with straw).

The outer walls are two and a half feet thick. They keep the building cool in summer and warm in winter.

The fort covers an area more than half the length of a football field. Clustered around the inner courtyard are about thirty rooms, on two levels. Among the most interesting are the kitchen, dining room, trade room and blacksmith shop. Here you can see a real blacksmith at work. The trading room has beaver pelts, buffalo robes, tallow candles and other old-fashioned goods.

Standing in the center of the courtyard is an interesting fur press. This was used to pack down beaver pelts and other skins before shipping them to far away St. Louis. A horse corral is in back. Prickly, needle-sharp cacti planted along the edge of the roof keep off "raiding Indians"!

Above the big front gate sits the belfry. From here a loud tolling bell once called people to meals. High over the fort the American flag flies again—today with fifty stars.

There's a walk along the rooftop where you can inspect the watchtowers and gaze out over the Colorado countryside. You might even pretend to spot some Indians or a herd of roaming buffalo!

State of Colorado

Aerial view of Bent's reconstructed fort.

Little Chief
Earns His Name

Kit Carson rolled over and rubbed the sleep out of his eyes. Through the trees a cold, gray winter dawn was breaking. The campfire burned low. A dozen men, wrapped in buffalo robes, lay sprawled about it. Kit hated to wake them. All day yesterday they had worked hard cutting trees and hauling timber. Captain Bent was building a big trading fort, only a few miles away, down on the Arkansas River. Young Kit Carson was in charge of the logging crew, here on Wild Horse Creek.

Last night two Indians had come to visit the camp. Black Whiteman and Little Turtle were friendly Cheyennes. They were curious about the new fort where they would

Christopher (Kit) Carson, who ran away from home at 16 to become one of the best fur trappers, hunters, guides and soldiers in the West.

soon be coming to trade. They sat up late telling stories and smoking tobacco by the white man's fire. Now they, too, were sleeping peacefully.

Kit crawled out of his snug, warm robe. He stood up, stretched and looked around. Suddenly his eyes almost popped out of his head. All of the men's horses were missing! A party of unfriendly Crows must have stolen them in the night. Only the two Cheyenne Indian ponies were left. How stupid he had been to let Captain Bent's horses run loose, unguarded. But there was no time to regret his mistake now. The Captain would be furious if he did not recover the animals. Quickly he roused the men, telling them what had happened. "Grab your rifles, boys," he yelled. "We're going after those horse thieves!"

The men struck out on foot through the deep snow. Black Whiteman and Little Turtle went with them. Kit was thankful that the Cheyennes, at least, had had the sense last night to tie up their ponies. The two Indians rode out ahead, following the tracks made by the Crows. All day the little group marched north across the prairie. Wind whipped their faces and blowing snow stung them in the eyes. But they trudged on, mile after mile.

Night was falling when they saw some red sparks rise from a willow thicket. They were getting close! Kit gathered the men about him. "Circle around to the side of the thicket," he told Black Whiteman and Little Turtle. "Then while we attack, you drive off the horses."

The two Cheyennes rode off quietly. Kit's men spread out in a long line, side by side. They all dropped to the ground. Slowly they crept forward on their hands and knees. They were almost to the edge of the thicket when a dog barked loudly. Seconds later a white puff of steam rose above the trees. The Crows were dumping snow on their fire. They must have seen them! The men hurried forward.

Suddenly a swarm of warriors came whooping out of the willows. There were at least sixty of them. They carried bows and arrows and wore long, sharp knives. The white men quickly dodged behind trees and bushes. When Kit gave the order, they raised their rifles and fired. Two Indians fell dead. The rest fled back into the trees. Kit and his men charged after them. The Crows raced to the spot where they had left the horses. But the animals had disappeared! The frightened Indians ran on through the thicket and out the other side. They streaked over the prairie as fast as they could go.

The men did not try to follow. They rolled in the snow, laughing and panting. Presently they heard a sound that was, indeed, sweet music to their ears. It was the gentle whinny of a horse! "Come on, boys!" called Kit. "They're down by the creek!" They ran down to where Black Whiteman and Little Turtle were waiting. Sure enough, there were the missing horses. How happy the men were

Colorado Historical Society

Drawing of Kit Carson guiding John Charles Fremont on one of his western expeditions.

to see them! The horses were happy too. They butted the men playfully with their heads.

Next morning the party started back for the logging camp. Black Whiteman and Little Turtle said good-bye. Then they found the two dead Crows and scalped them. They rode off in haste to rejoin the Cheyennes. How pleased Chief Yellow Wolf would be with their bloody trophies! They could hardly wait to tell him how Kit Carson, with only a dozen men, had chased away sixty Crows!

A few days later Chief Yellow Wolf visited Captain Bent. Kit Carson was there. The three men sat smoking together in the council room of the half built fort. Yellow Wolf questioned Kit about the fight. "How is it," he asked, "that thirteen mighty firesticks shoot two Crows? This very low war count, little white man."

Kit felt his face grow hot. The Chief was making fun of him! He hung his head in shame. Yellow Wolf rose slowly to his feet. He drew his buffalo robe about him. Then he raised his right hand and held it over Kit's head. "Little white man have big courage," he said solemnly. "With few palefaces you scare many Crows. I give you a new name. You have earned it. From now on my people will call you Vih-hiu-nis—Little Chief of the Cheyennes."

Kit could hardly believe his ears. Little Chief! And a moment ago he had thought he was being laughed at. Kit looked up at Yellow Wolf. "I am honored," he said. "I will try to be a good chief."

Yellow Wolf grinned. "You very brave," he said. "But smart chief remember next time to tie horses!"

Kit never again forgot.

* * * *

Kit Carson's life was as exciting as Daniel Boone's. His boyhood was spent on the Missouri frontier. Schools were few in those days and Kit never learned to read or write. But he was wise in the ways of the woods. He could ride, and shoot, and track wild animals like an Indian.

Kit's father died when he was nine. At fifteen, his mother forced him to go to work for a saddle maker. But Kit did not like making saddles. He longed to be outdoors in the sunshine. So at sixteen he ran away from home. He joined Charles Bent's wagon train, headed west for Santa Fe. (The saddle maker offered a one cent reward for Kit's capture. Nobody, of course, ever collected it!)

Kit never grew to be very tall. But what he lacked in size he made up for in courage. Once two grizzly bears chased him up a tree. He fended them off with only his hunting knife! Kit trapped beaver all over the Rockies. In time he became one of the most famous mountain men of the west.

Although he sometimes had to fight them, Kit Carson admired the Indians. It made him sad to see them forced from their lands by the white man. Kit was especially friendly with the Indians of the plains. Two of his wives belonged to these tribes. The first was an Arapahoe woman named "Waa-nibe," or "Grass Singing." Kit fought a duel to win her. After she died he married a Cheyenne woman called "Making Out the Road." Kit Carson's third and last wife was a beautiful Spanish girl named Josepha Jaramillo (Ho-see-fah Har-ah-me-yo).

Kit Carson did not spend his whole life trapping. When people stopped wearing beaver hats, he found other things to do. For a while he became a buffalo hunter, supplying meat to Bent's Fort. Then he served as guide to Captain John Charles Fremont, who explored parts of Oregon and California. Kit fought in both the war against Mexico and the Civil War. In between these wars he was an Indian agent in Taos, New Mexico. He tried hard to bring about understanding between whites and Indians.

Although Kit Carson's home was in Taos, he spent much of his time in Colorado. A town, a county, a mountain and an army post (Fort Carson) are named for him. He died at Fort Lyon, Colorado, in 1868. The last words he whispered to his doctor were "adios, compadre— good-bye, friend."

Engines Under the Snow

Do you ever ski at Winter Park, just over the mountains from Denver? If you do, you probably ride the ski train that goes through the Moffat Tunnel. It's always fun to zip through this dark, scary tunnel. But did you realize that it passes under the Continental Divide? Before the tunnel was built, trains had to climb to more than two miles above sea level to cross over Rollins Pass.

Of course in those days trains didn't carry skiers. They hauled only such necessary things as lumber, cattle and coal. People rode the train up in the summertime to hike and picnic. But during the winter blizzards, in thirty-below zero weather, there were few passengers riding over the pass!

Locomotives did not burn diesel fuel as they do today, either. They were run by steam. The sweating fireman shoveled coal into the firebox, which heated up water in the boiler. If you've ever watched something boil over on the stove, you know that steam can push the lid off a pot. Now in a steam engine, this steam power was used to push pistons back and forth, which in turn drove the wheels. The following story tells what happened to a train crossing the Rockies one day in February, 1905.

The train started up the mountain that morning from Tolland, a stop just east of the Divide. A huge snowplow called "The Monster Termite" was hooked up ahead of the two engines. The Termite's job was to chew through the great snowdrifts with its sharp, spinning blades. Trainmen called it a "rotary" because the big blades spun around like a fan, throwing snow far and wide. When the train reached Jenny Lake, the wind was roaring off the Divide like a runaway engine. This was the last water stop until they were over the pass, so the crew filled up the tanks.

Now began the hardest part of the climb. Up and up they puffed, fighting their way through the heavy twelve-

Rotary crew stops to probe for rock covering tracks on the Moffat "Hell Hill" Line. Badly cut up blades often had to be rebuilt.

foot drifts. The tracks wound in and out like a giant snake wrapping itself around the mountain. It was only about four miles to the top. But the Termite was using up valuable steam energy with every turn of the blades. The men began to worry about their water. Barely creeping, the locomotives pulled up the last 200 feet. Here they crawled into the snowshed (a kind of giant, wooden house built over the tracks) at Rollins Pass.

Smoke from the engines filled the shed, stinging the men's eyes and blackening their faces. The sooty air made them cough and choke. The men measured their water in the tanks behind the engines. It was dangerously low. But fortunately, they were now headed downhill. Besides, they could always shovel snow into the tanks if they ran out of water.

The train pulled out of the big shed, slowly picking up speed. Soon it was going about nine miles an hour. How the wind howled out of the valley below! Was it trying to blow them back up the pass? Passengers buttoned up their coats as the snow sifted in through the windows. Belching smoke, the train chugged along for a mile and a half. Then suddenly, it stopped. Sure enough, the engines were out of water. The men climbed up on the tenders and began to shovel. But the wind blew the snow away as fast as they could collect it. It was no use. They were hopelessly stalled, in a raging blizzard.

The conductor told his seven passengers to "hit the cinders" (walk out) while they could still follow the tracks down the mountain. Since they were all tough lumberjacks and ranchers, he knew they would make it down safely. Meanwhile the brakeman started back afoot to Rollins Pass to get help. Battling the storm, he staggered back up into the snowshed. There, a telegraph operator called Tolland to order up two new engines. These would be used to pull the stranded train back into the snowshed.

Meanwhile, back at the train, the conductor had climbed a telegraph pole. Using a special key, he sent a dot-and-dash message to Denver. Here is what it said: "Engines gone dead due to low water. Can't shovel snow in the terrible gale." Night was coming on now, and the men were getting hungry. In the freight car they found canned goods, frozen potatoes and several quarters of beef. These supplies were bound for the sawmill at Arrowhead. But the stranded men had to eat. So they cut up the beef with one of the axes they found in a tool box. They thawed the frozen potatoes and cooked them on the caboose stove. Then to help pass the long night, they began playing cards and telling stories.

Moffat Line loops around Yankee Doodle Lake below James Peak.
Train at top right has just passed through Needle's Eye Tunnel.

By next morning the two rescue engines had reached Rollins Pass. But in the struggle up the mountain, they too had run out of water. They would not be able to rescue the stalled train. A second stormy day passed. The weary men fired the engines just enough to keep them from freezing. Every drop of water was becoming precious.

By the third day, the train was almost buried in the snowdrifts. Realizing that they would not be rescued soon, the crew decided to walk out. They left the train and started off together in the storm. The snow was so deep that they could only find their way by following the telegraph lines.

As they approached the pass, they saw something black sticking above the snow. It was the top of the workmen's cook car! The snowed-in track workers had fitted seven

With rotary blades spinning, a snowplow chews through heavy winter drifts on Rollins Pass. Three rotary plows kept the hill open.

pieces of stovepipe together to make it reach high enough. The men came down through the skylight and were treated by the cook to some biscuits. Then they walked on through the shed.

Coming out, they looked down on frozen Yankee Doodle Lake, 1,000 feet below. Suddenly, one of them decided to take a shortcut. Jumping on his coal shovel, he shot to the bottom like a bullet. But he burned the seat of his pants off on the way! His less daring comrades kept trudging along the tracks. At Jenny Lake Boxcar, they telegraphed Tolland: "NINE EXTRAS EAST, LIGHT." Can you figure out what they said? Yes, they meant that nine people were traveling east on foot.

At Tolland a hot dinner was waiting for the men. They were almost 3,000 feet lower now and safely out of the storm. But what of the stalled train? Well, the story has a happy ending. Finally, the Moffat train was rescued by two engines and a snowplow borrowed from another railroad. But first the giant drifts had to be blasted loose with dynamite. The rescue engines hauled the train west to Arrowhead, where the lumber camp was happy to receive its supplies. They hardly noticed that some of their food was missing! And what about the nine men who had tramped over the Continental Divide? They were so dirty and bearded that their families back in Denver hardly recognized them. But they must have had a happy reunion!

* * * *

This story is just one of many about the Moffat "Hell Hill" line, as it was called. The railroad men also battled fires, derailments and snowslides. They were mighty happy when the Moffat Tunnel was completed through the mountains in 1927. If only pioneer David Moffat could have lived to see it! For now his dream of putting Denver on a speedy transcontinental railroad route would come true.

Trains do not run over Rollins Pass anymore. But you can follow the old railroad grade by car. The bumpy gravel road winds up past beautiful Yankee Doodle and Jenny Lakes. Then it passes through Needle's Eye Tunnel and crosses two high, scary trestles. At the top are huge piles of rotting timbers. These are all that is left of the old snowshed, railroad ties and telegraph poles. Not far away is the crumbling brick foundation of an old hotel. Close your eyes and listen. Perhaps in the stillness, you'll hear the ghostly whistle of a steam engine tooting around the bend!

Colorado's Most Daring Skier

Can you imagine skiing alone at night over Colorado's high mountain passes—with thirty pounds on your back and only one ski pole? Sounds unbelievable, doesn't it? But that is what Father John Lewis Dyer, Colorado's first cross-country skier, did time and again. Father Dyer didn't ski for fun. He was a pioneer minister who brought both God's word and the weekly mail to remote mining camps. He skied at night because the snow was firmer and safer then.

Father Dyer was born and raised in the Midwest. Suddenly, at age forty-nine, he thought he was going blind. So he decided to see Pikes Peak while he still had his sight. Joining a wagon train in Nebraska (which gave him food only), Father Dyer walked the 600 miles to Denver. He arrived so poor that he had to swap his watch for something to eat! With only a buffalo robe for a bedroll, he set out next day for the mining country.

Back in the 1860s people were too busy digging for gold to build churches. But they gathered eagerly in stores, gambling houses and saloons to hear Father Dyer. Unfortunately, they were not able to pay him very much. So when he wasn't preaching, he earned a little extra money by carrying mail. Every week, in all kinds of weather, he traveled up over 13,180 foot high Mosquito Pass, from Buckskin Joe to the Leadville mining area. He also carried the miner's gold dust to Denver, where it was exchanged for paper money, gold coin or silver.

Father Dyer had never heard of skis, so he called his homemade wooden carriers "snowshoes." In this story we'll call them skis, which they really were. You wouldn't have enjoyed skiing on them, however. They were ten feet long, about ten inches wide, and were held on with only a toe strap! He used his single pole for knocking snow off their bottoms.

One night Father Dyer was traveling from Fairplay to Oro City, near Leadville. While skiing along the bank of the Platte River, he passed over some willows buried under the snow. Crunch! The sound of splintering wood told him he'd broken one of his skis. Oh, well—he'd manage somehow. Taking off his boots and socks, he waded across the icy brook. His feet were now freezing cold. With his remaining ski, he scraped away the loose snow to make a place to stamp his feet on. They soon warmed up, and after resting for awhile, he went on.

But when he got above timberline, the fresh powder would not hold him up on his one ski. He could only go about three steps before sinking in snow up to his waist. He knew he was in serious trouble. Traveling this slowly, he could easily freeze to death.

It was about midnight when he reached the top of Mosquito Pass. The lights of Oro City twinkled far below him in the gulch. But how could he possibly make it that far with a thirty-pound mail bag and only one ski? Off to the north he noticed a shadowy grove of pine trees. They were not on his route. But if he could reach them he might be able to build a fire.

There was no time to lose. Praying that wild beasts would not disturb it, he set the bulging mail sack down in the snow. Then rolling and crawling, he dragged himself over into the timber. He found a dry stump and soon had a roaring fire. Taking off his mittens, he spread his hands before it. How good the blessed warmth felt on his numb, half frozen fingers! He knelt in the snow and thanked God.

Then he made a bed out of some pine boughs and lay down under the stars. They seemed to be crowding around to keep him company on that high, lonely mountain. Far away in the distance an owl hooted. Then some wolves began to howl. Father Dyer started singing a hymn. His mighty voice filled the woods and echoed across the mountains. The wolves and the owl were soon stilled, and the exhausted minister dropped off to sleep.

When he awoke it was daylight. He wondered if the snow had frozen hard enough to walk on. He crawled onto it carefully and stood up. It held! Carrying his single ski, he backtracked to where he'd left the mail sack. It was untouched, but the wolves had beaten a path all around it in the snow. How close they had come! Slinging the mail over his back, he made his way on down the mountain. When he got to Oro City he stopped at the home of a friend. There he ate a huge breakfast of antelope stew. How relieved he was to have the night's adventures behind him!

* * * *

Father Dyer had many other adventures. Once he fell over a cliff in a blizzard. Another time an avalanche just missed him. Later on in life he moved to Breckenridge where he helped build a little wooden church which is still being used today. But Father Dyer would recognize little else in Breckenridge if he could come back for a visit. How shocked he would be to see skiers instead of gold hunters swarming all over the mountains. But it would probably please him very much to see his face pictured on one of the stained glass windows of our State Capitol dome. This pioneer preacher and mail carrier did much to help settle Colorado.

Western History Department, Denver Public Library

Rev. John L. Dyer

The River of Death

Not many people live in the northwestern corner of Colorado. This desert-like part of our state is a land of deep canyons and swiftly flowing rivers. Jack-rabbits and antelopes run freely through the sagebrush while snakes and lizards scamper across the sand.

Near the Utah border is a place called Lodore Canyon. The rocky walls of this canyon are high and steep. In 1869 a bearded man with only one arm climbed to the top of them. From the canyon's rim, he looked down 2,000 feet to the Green River. The ribbon of water far below him glimmered in the sunlight. He thought of the mysterious tales he had heard about it. The Ute Indians called it the "River of Death." They would not go near its banks. "Rocks h-e-a-p high," one old Indian told him. "Water pony h-e-a-p buck. Who go on death river not come back. Water catch 'em."

He wondered if the Indian's warnings were true. Further on did the Green River have falls as high as Niagara? And were there places where it plunged underground and disappeared? Nobody knew because no one had ever explored it all. No one, that is, until now. For the one-armed man, along with nine companions, was going down this river.

His name was John Wesley Powell. He was an army man, geologist, teacher and explorer. He had lost his right arm during a battle in the Civil War. But this didn't stop him from setting forth on one of the greatest explorations in America's history. He and his men were boating down the Green River, all the way from southern Wyoming to the end of the Grand Canyon. If they came out alive, they would be the first people ever to do so. And if they did not . . . well, this was simply a risk they would have to take. For Major Powell was determined to learn the truth about this river and its canyons. He must know why it cut through mountains instead of going around them. And he must find the place where it and the Grand came together to form the mighty Colorado.

Next morning, after a breakfast of bacon and biscuits, the men set off through Lodore Canyon. They traveled in four wooden boats. They were much heavier than the river running rafts of today. In them they carried food, guns, camping equipment and Powell's scientific instruments. Powell's boat, the *Emma Dean*, pushed off first. The other three boats came bouncing along behind. For several hours they raced along over the smooth water.

Then, rounding a bend, they approached some rapids. Powell headed for the shore, signalling the other boats to follow. He planned to walk along the bank, looking for a place to get through. If he found an opening they would shoot the rapids. But if he did not it would mean hard work for the men. For then they would have to pass the boats down on ropes, or carry them along the shore.

The *Kitty Clyde's Sister* followed the *Emma Dean* to safety. After them came the *Maid of the Canyon*. Then, a minute later, Powell heard a shout. As he turned around he saw the *No Name* go plunging past. Either they had missed the landing signal or had seen it too late. For they were headed straight into the rapids.

Their friends ran after them along the shore. But there was nothing they could do. They watched helplessly as the boat swept over a ten-foot waterfall, down onto the murderous rocks below. It struck a great boulder and was

State of Colorado

Green River in northwestern corner of Colorado, flowing peacefully
into Lodore Canyon above Disaster Falls where Powell was wrecked.

flipped into the air. The three men were flung out like flies.
Their heads bobbed above the swirling water. The boat,
which had gotten stuck on the rocks, was not far away.

They managed to climb back in—and just in time. For
soon the boat worked itself loose and went spinning madly
on. The men clung tightly to the sides, as the boat, now
half full of water, tossed about in the foam. They heard the
thundering roar of more rapids ahead. Then they were in
them. There was a mighty C-R-A-C-K as the boat crashed
broadside into another boulder. The heavy oak vessel
snapped in two like a matchstick. Once more the men

77

Powell's party at Green River Station, Wyoming, before setting
off to conquer the untamed Green-Colorado, the river of death.

were flung into the angry torrent. And this time it looked
like they must surely drown or be beaten to death on the
rocks.

But luck was with them. Two of the men were washed
up onto a stony island. The third man, his head barely
above water, clung to a jagged rock nearby. Using an oar
from the boat, his buddies hauled him up onto the island.
For the time being, at least, the three men were safe. But
they couldn't stay on the island forever. Someone would
have to rescue them. Major Powell, with only one arm,
could not do it. So he sent another man out in the *Emma
Dean*. Powell watched anxiously as the little boat fought its
way through the boiling rapids. At last it reached the tip of
the island. The men climbed aboard and began another
wild ride. But this time they were headed for the shore and
safety.

There was great rejoicing when the men reached the bank. They were soaked through and exhausted—but they were alive! Their companions pounded them gleefully on the back. But the excitement faded as the men began to realize their plight. The loss of the boat was serious. Almost a third of their food and equipment had been swept down the river. Worst of all was the loss of Major Powell's barometers. These glass tubes filled with mercury were his most valuable instruments. Without them he would not be able to measure the depths of the canyons they passed through. Much scientific work would go undone.

Next morning the Major and his men walked along the shore. They were looking for the splintered remains of the *No Name*. Before long they spotted the stern half of the boat. It lay jammed up against some rocks in the middle of the river. Two men got in the *Emma Dean* and rowed over to the wreck. They poked about for a few moments. Then they shouted excitedly and waved their arms. They had found the barometers! They still lay in their package unbroken!

The two men also brought back some thermometers and a keg of whiskey. But they were unable to salvage any of the food or clothing. And the party had hundreds of miles to travel through unknown country. Would they come out alive? Or would they drown, starve or perhaps freeze to death? What lay ahead? Nobody knew. Their death-defying adventure on the Green-Colorado had just begun!

* * * *

Three months later Powell and five of his men did come out alive. But conquering the Green-Colorado had not been easy. The river did not run underground anywhere, and there were no falls as high as Niagara. Nevertheless, the men had many hair-raising adventures along that untamed waterway. Once they barely escaped from a raging fire along the river bank. And twice, while exploring high in the canyon, the one-armed Major nearly plummeted to his death. (The place in the canyon where the *No Name* was wrecked they called "Disaster Falls." Today, in rubber rafts and kayaks, people ride over these same thrilling rapids.)

The river was not all they had to contend with. Toward the end of the trip their food began to run out. Rancid bacon, soggy apples, and moldy flour were all the starving men had to eat. And the rapids kept getting worse. At the end of the Grand Canyon they came to the scariest rapids of all. Three men refused to go on. They left the party and climbed up out of the canyon. Their six companions plunged ahead. The next day they found themselves in quieter water. They had made it through! But the three deserters were not so lucky. After scaling the mile high cliffs they were killed by Indians.

Powell learned many things on this trip. He discovered, for instance, that mountains were not always formed before rivers. Some rivers were formed before mountains. The Green-Colorado was one of these. Millions of years ago, before there were any mountains, it flowed through flat country. Then as the land rose up, the river cut its way down through the earth. It actually sawed the mountains in two. Eventually it cut so deep that it formed the Grand Canyon.

Powell found the place (in Utah) where the Green and the Grand Rivers came together to form the Colorado River. The Grand River no longer exists. Its name has been changed to the upper Colorado. It has its beginnings in Grand Lake in Rocky Mountain National Park.

Today the Colorado is one of the most important rivers in the United States. In the dry, desert-like Southwest, water is more precious than gold. The Colorado River supplies millions of people living in several western states. Huge dams have been built to store the water. Farmers use some of it to irrigate their crops. Thirsty cities take more. And some of the water spins giant wheels which produce electricity to light homes and run factories. The mighty Colorado has truly become a river of life.

U.S. Geological Survey

One-armed John Wesley Powell chatting with a Paiute Indian.

A Lady Climbs a Mountain

Would you climb a 14,256-foot mountain in a long skirt, bloomers, and men's hunting boots several sizes too large for you? That is how Isabella Bird was dressed when she started up Longs Peak with fierce looking Rocky Mountain Jim, back in 1873. She didn't even carry water! Miss Bird was an English lady who traveled and wrote books. Her back often hurt, but that did not stop her from riding horses or climbing mountains. Before coming to Colorado she camped out in Hawaii, near the edge of a volcano.

Her adventures in the Rocky Mountains were no less daring. Alone, without even a compass to guide her, she rode her little horse, Birdie, over prairies and high mountain passes. She liked lonely mountain trails the best. Here she could sit comfortably astride. Before coming to a town, however, she had to fasten a skirt over her bloomers and ride side saddle. In those days it was thought unladylike to straddle a horse!

Isabella spent most of her time in and around Estes Park, her favorite part of Colorado. Of course there was no town there over 100 years ago. When people talked about Estes Park they meant the high mountain valley, ringed by peaks. Only a handful of people lived in the area. One of them was Jim Nugent, a mountain man who had a small log cabin.

One-eyed Rocky Mountain Jim fascinated Isabella. The right side of his face had been clawed by a grizzly bear. But the left side was still handsome. Many people were afraid of him because he sometimes got drunk and did terrible things. It was even whispered that he had once killed a man! But this did not bother Miss Bird. She treated the trapper kindly, and he was always polite and courteous to her in return. On their long rides together, he told her Indian tales. He even recited his own poetry.

Even since coming to the park, Isabella had wanted to climb its highest peak. She would gaze up at it longingly from her cabin on the Griff Evans ranch. But could she do it? Isabella decided to try. She hired Rocky Mountain Jim as her guide. Two young men went with them. The first night the party camped out at the foot of the peak. The next morning they rode off early. Jim wore a ragged leather shirt and deerhide trousers, held up by a scarf. An old hat was smashed down over his tangled curls. With a knife in his belt, pistol in his pocket, and patch over his eye, he looked fierce as a pirate! But he behaved, as always, like a perfect gentleman. Miss Bird wore her long skirt and bloomers. On her feet were a pair of Mr. Evans's hunting boots.

At the end of the trail they dismounted and tied their horses. In front of them loomed the peak, its smooth wall of granite slicing the sky. To reach it they had to scramble across a field of huge boulders. Isabella kept tripping in Mr. Evans's big, floppy boots. All at once she spied something under a rock. It was a pair of ladies' overshoes! They must have been left there just last month by Anna Dickinson, first woman to climb Longs Peak. Isabella tried them on and they fit. Now she hopped easily from rock to rock.

Ahead of them was a jagged hole in the side of the mountain. It looked as if a giant had bitten a chunk right out of the rim. As they approached, the hole got bigger and bigger. Soon they found themselves climbing up into it. Then they stepped right through it. Now they were on the other side of the mountain. Snowy peaks rose all about them. Far below, little bluegreen lakes lay tucked away in the pines. Above them towered 2,000 feet of solid rock. Isabella was terrified. She begged Jim to leave her behind. But he refused. "You are going up this mountain even if I have to carry you," he told her.

Roped to Jim, Isabella began the climb. Falling rocks bruised her ankles. Her arms felt like they were being pulled from their sockets. But Jim dragged her on. In the steep places he made "steps" for her with his feet and hands. The sharp mountain air cut like a knife through Isabella's thin riding dress. Her heart was pounding like a hammer, and her lungs felt as if they would burst.

Western History Department, Denver Public Library

Isabella Lucy Bird and her little horse, Birdie.

After reaching the top of a deep ravine, they passed under a narrow, overhanging ledge. Isabella clung tightly to Jim as they crawled along. She didn't dare look down. One careless step and she would go spinning dizzily to her death, 3,000 feet below. Suddenly they turned a corner and saw the top of the peak. They began inching their way up the last 500 feet. All they had to hang on to were narrow cracks in the walls. Isabella felt like a tiny ant scaling a brick wall.

But at last they were on top. Endless plains stretched to the horizon while far off mountain ranges played "tag" with the clouds. They could see the hazy outline of Pikes Peak—more than 100 miles away. But they didn't stop long to enjoy the view. Breathing was difficult in the high, thin air. One of the young men's lungs was bleeding. Isabella was so thirsty that her tongue rattled around in her mouth. After leaving their names and the date in a tin can, they started down. Jim went first so that Isabella could brace her feet against his shoulders. Once she caught her dress on a rock and hung helplessly in the air. Jim had to cut her loose with his hunting knife.

Finally they were down. They stood for awhile watching the purple sun dip below the plains. Then they rode back to camp. Isabella was so tired that she almost fell asleep on her horse. Jim built a roaring fire. Then he tucked Isabella into her blankets. Soon she was fast asleep, dreaming of the terrible peak.

* * * *

Longs Peak is now part of Rocky Mountain National Park. It was named for Stephen H. Long, army man and explorer. But he was not the first person to climb the mountain. In fact he never climbed it at all. He didn't even discover it. French traders and trappers were probably the first white people to see the peak. They named Longs, and its lower sister peak, Mt. Meeker, "The Two Ears." The Indians, even earlier, had called them "The Two Guides." They used them as a landmark to help find their way. They also climbed the mountains to trap eagles.

Although Major Long did not climb or even discover the peak, he was the first person to *write* about it. That is why it is named for him. In the summer of 1820, Long led twenty-two men on horseback along the front range of the

Chasm Lake below shee east face of Long's Pea

Rockies. Two dogs, which were with the party, died of thirst on the plains. Major Long did not think much of eastern Colorado. He called it "The Great American Desert," and said that nobody would ever live there. Lieutenant Pike thought the same thing. Wouldn't they be surprised today!

The peak which bears Long's name, was climbed for the first time in 1868. This was almost fifty years after his expedition through what is now Colorado. Major John Wesley Powell, a man with only one arm, led six people to the summit. Since Isabella Bird's trip in 1873, thousands have climbed the peak. Rock climbers on ropes have even gone straight up over the east face. But most people still follow Isabella's route. Today we call this approach "The Keyhole." Can you figure out why? (The spot below timberline where Isabella and Jim camped out is now called "Jim's Grove.")

People are a lot more sensible about climbing than they were 100 years ago. We now wear sturdy boots and take along plenty of warm clothing and water. No one would dream of wearing a dress. But people still do reckless things. Part way up the mountain stands a little stone hut. It was built in memory of a woman who lost her life trying to climb the icy east face in winter. A few other people have been killed by lightning or falling rocks.

But most people make it safely to the summit. In 1927 a couple were even married in a snowstorm on top of Longs! Eighty-five year olds have climbed the famous mountain—and so have five-year old children. Maybe you'll conquer this "fourteener" yourself, someday!

Canaries, Rats, Mules, Miners and Tommyknockers

As you hike or drive around Colorado, you see many old tunnels and deserted mine diggings. Here, men once swarmed over the mountains like ants, looking for silver and gold. Imagine what it must have been like going to work in a mine over 100 years ago.

First the miner climbed into a big, steel bucket. Then by means of a "donkey engine," he was lowered hundreds of feet into the earth. This little "workhorse" engine powered a long cable which hoisted the bucket up and down. Later, Colorado miners went down in an elevator with bars all around called a "cage." But the early day bucket was scary indeed to ride in.

After dropping to the bottom of the narrow shaft, the miners picked up their tools. Then they went to work in a damp, smelly tunnel. Water dripped everywhere. It was so black that the men could scarcely see their hands before their faces. That is why they carried candles, or later wore tiny oil lamps on their caps. One man would hold a big, steel drill, while his partner hammered it into the rocks. The sweating pair then filled the hole with dynamite and blasted out the rich ore.

Even though the miners were used to working underground they could never relax and feel safe. Sudden cave-ins often trapped the men, or falling rocks crushed them to death. Fires and accidents were common. And sometimes a careless miner slipped and fell screaming down the shaft.

Colorado Historical Society

Small wonder Colorado's hardrock miners were nervous on the job! People who live in constant danger develop strange habits. They try to keep from having bad luck by doing or not doing certain things. We call such people superstitious (su-per-stish-us). Not surprisingly, the early day miners of Colorado had many superstitions.

They believed, for example, that accidents always happened in threes; that it was bad luck for a woman to enter a mine; that it was dangerous to whistle underground; and that a man was likely to fall if his work clothes slipped off their hook on the wall. They even thought it a sign of bad luck for a miner to drop his tools in the mine.

Several of their strongest superstitions were about candles. Miners believed that if a candle fell from the tunnel wall or went out three times, something was wrong at home. They never lit each other's candles. Passing a light from one person to another might, they feared, take the "life" out of it. And miners had good reason to fear a candle flickering out—for often it meant the presence of poisonous gasses. That is why the miners sometimes took canaries into the mines. The delicate birds could not breathe long in bad air. When his canary died, a miner knew it was time to get out of the mine.

Miners treasured rats, too. They never shot them, for these ugly little rodents seemed able to sense danger. The miners had a saying: "When the rats move out, so does the miner." And the rats did lead many a miner to safety, just before a cave-in or an explosion. Sometimes they even alerted sleeping miners by tugging with their teeth on the men's clothes. No wonder they became pets.

The miner's mules were also sensitive to danger. One time, so the story goes, a mule started out of the tunnel before the ore car was filled. The miner followed, and he was mighty glad he did. For just after they'd left, the entire tunnel caved in! Even black cats and howling dogs were important to miners. A man meeting either of these "unlucky" animals on his way to work would probably turn around and go home.

Perhaps the miners' strangest belief of all had to do with amazing ghosts called Tommyknockers. These little men, who stood about two feet tall, were believed to be the spirits of dead miners. They had big heads, old, wrinkled faces, and long beards. Their arms reached nearly to the ground. The weird little sprites wore tiny miner's boots and colorful shirts.

But miners rarely saw the Tommyknockers. They just knew they were there because of their tap-tap-tapping on the walls. It was a very lucky miner who was awakened by a Tommyknocker between midnight and two in the morning. According to the superstition, he had only to follow the knocking to discover a rich vein of ore. If he lost the sound, the miner just tapped on the wall, and the Tommyknocker tapped back.

Like canaries and rats, Tommyknockers, too, sometimes saved the lives of miners. Once a miner stood on a rock in the middle of a deep pool of water. Suddenly, invisible hands pushed him hard from behind. Kerplunk! He splashed into the water. As he swam away, a huge boulder fell right on the spot where he'd been standing.

Although Tommyknockers were friendly little fellows, they did like to play tricks. Sometimes they would hide a miner's pick and shovel or upset his lunch bucket. Miners tried to keep their good will by sharing food with the playful creatures. They never shouted at or cursed the Tommyknockers. For if ignored or mistreated, the little spirits would turn spiteful. They might scamper up a ladder, kicking out the rungs as they went, so as to trap the helpless miners below. Or they could cause a small cave-in, burying tools and valuable ore.

Some people claimed that the ghostly tapping was heard only in places where miners had been killed. The dead men's restless spirits, they believed, were still trying to dig themselves out. Do you agree with this little poem about a Tommyknocker?

> Knock, knock
> Tap, tap
> What's that sound?
> 'Tis the soul of a miner locked deep in the ground.
> He'll knock that way till the end of time.
> For he's buried 'neath a mountain of muck and slime.
>
> Knock, knock
> Tap, tap
> Who goes there?
> 'Tis a Tommyknocker knockin' on the midnight air!
> The sound of his tapping will serve, no doubt,
> To warn other miners that they'd better get OUT!

Stampede!

The air was hot and sticky that August night over 100 years ago. Not a blade of grass was stirring on the Colorado prairies. Far away on the horizon pink flashes lighted up the sky. Thunder rumbled faintly. A thousand Longhorn cattle lay dozing in the darkness, their bellies bulging with fresh grass and water. Two cowboys slowly circled the sprawling herd. They eyed the bedded down cattle nervously as a coyote howled in the distance. As

An old 1881 drawing of cowboys circling thunder-frightened stampeding cattle along the Texas Trail to Colorado.

"night riders," their job was to see that no sudden noise startled the sleeping animals. Their voices mingled with the dying echo of the coyote's call as they sang softly:

> Ride around the little dogies
> Ride around 'em slow
> For the fieries and snuffies
> Are rarin' to go . . . .

The serenading stopped for a moment as the cowboys pulled their horses together. "They're sure layin' quiet," drawled Sam.

"Too quiet," replied Bill. "I like steers to lie still all right. But I expect to hear 'em switchin' their tails and blowin' off a little as they settle down for the night. Them dogies are as silent as tombstones."

The lightning flared again, closer this time. In the flickering brightness the men could see that every steer's head was down.

"What time is it?" asked Sam.

Bill felt around in the dark and pulled a watch out of his pocket. He struck a match against the sole of his boot. Holding the light up close, he squinted at the time. "Half past nine," he answered.

"Only half an hour to go before the next guard comes on," said Sam. He yawned. "Guess I'll be ridin' along." He trotted away into the inky blackness.

Now the wind began to pick up and a tumbleweed rolled by. It brushed against Old Buck, lead steer on the Colorado trail. He lifted his head and looked around. Sniffing the air, he got on his feet and gazed toward the approaching storm. Another steer got up. Then another . . . and another. Soon, the whole herd was standing.

Bill's singing grew louder:

Oh bury me not
On the lone prairie
Where the coyotes howl
And the wind blows free . . .

But it was no use. His voice was lost on the rising wind. The cattle began to sway. Ghostly lights flashed on the tips of their waving horns. Foxfire! An electric storm was on the way! The steers started milling around in a circle. Then they moved faster. A great fork of lightning zigzagged down through the sky. Then a deafening thunderclap jarred the heavens.

All at once, thousands of pounding hoofs hit the prairie. Back in camp, the sleeping cowboys tumbled out of their

bedrolls. They grabbed their ponies and raced after the stampeding herd. Galloping in the lead, Bill and Sam tried to head off the snorting, plunging Longhorns. Up and down gullies and across dry stream beds they raced. Their surefooted horses managed somehow to miss the prairie dog holes. Landing in one of these could easily have broken a horse's leg or thrown a cowboy. Rain slashed down in torrents. The heavens crashed around them, drowning out the noise of the thundering herd.

Bill and Sam were slowly gaining on them. If one rider could only pull far enough ahead, he might be able to turn the stampeding animals. Spurring his horse to the limit, Bill managed at last to pull alongside the lead steer, Old Buck.

"Turn him!" yelled Sam. "Turn him!"

Just then another bolt of lightning tore open the skies. Sam's horse, Cyclone, stopped dead in his tracks. Sam almost flew over his head. In the blinding flash, the cowboy saw that Cyclone's feet were planted on the edge of a high, steep river bank. Nearby, Bill was slumped over in his saddle, his head hanging low. Sam rushed over to his buddy, who had been stunned by the lightning. Meanwhile, the stampeding herd charged over the steep bank and into the river. While Sam helped Bill, the other cowboys followed the Longhorns across. A great many steers were drowned as they piled up in the churning water. The bawling of the terrified animals echoed eerily above the storm.

But the rushing river had broken the stampede. After climbing the opposite bank, the exhausted herd began to slow down. With much snorting and huffing the Longhorns came to a stop at last. Almost as quickly as it had begun, the stampede was over.

Back in camp next morning, the sleepless cowboys gathered around the chuckwagon for breakfast. Over sourdough flapjacks, bacon and strong, black coffee, they recalled their wild night. They had lost many valuable steers and a lot of money for the owners. But they were thankful that no one had been injured or killed. Sam was still shaking his head over his close call with the lightning. He hoped that the weather would be better along the rest of the trail to Denver!

* * * *

You won't find this exact story in the Colorado history books. But that doesn't mean it didn't happen. Lightning caused many stampedes much like this one. The early day cowboys just didn't have the time or energy to write about them. They told many stories, however.

The 1870s and 1880s were the years of the great western cattle drives. The miners, settlers and soldiers who poured into Colorado needed meat. So the Longhorn cattle were driven all the way from Texas, up through New Mexico and into Colorado. Crossing the plains, they passed just east of Pueblo, Colorado Springs and Denver. The horns of these amazing animals measured eight feet across from tip to tip!

Except for a few animals in zoos and rodeos, the Longhorns disappeared many years ago. The days of stampedes and cattle drives are gone forever. New short-horned breeds of cattle provide the beef for our tables today. They are speedily shipped to market by train and truck. Next time you bite into a juicy hamburger, think about the exciting adventures of the old time Colorado cowboys!

The Little Engineer Who Did

In southern Colorado, high in the San Juan mountains, is a town called Silverton. It is an old mining town where silver was once hauled out by the ton.

That is why the miners named it Silverton. Today a winding mountain highway passes through this sleepy little town. But in the old days it could only be reached by train.

Western History Department, Denver Public Library

Otto Mears

The railroad tracks ran along the steep sides of a mountain high above the Animas River. Now tracks are usually four feet, 8½ inches wide. But because there had been so little room to build them, these mountain tracks were only three feet apart. Little black engines pulling wooden coaches chugged up the canyon from Durango, over these narrow-gauge tracks. Every day, in all kinds of weather, they tooted their way up steep grades and around sharp, hairpin curves. The people depended on them to haul in food and supplies and haul out rich ore.

Then one day in 1911, the little trains stopped running. The Animas River had flooded its banks, washing out several miles of track. The twisted rails looked like pretzels piled along the river bank. It was October, and winter comes early to the high country. New tracks would have to be laid quickly.

But the Denver and Rio Grande Railroad had no extra coal with which to fire the work trains. Nor did any of the other railroads from whom the D. and R.G. tried to borrow. They had about given up hope of repairing the tracks when a little old gentleman with a white beard stepped forward. He was wearing a tall, silk hat.

"I think I can supply the coal for the work trains," he told the owners of the railroad. "In a few days I will have it for you."

The Denver and Rio Grande people were puzzled. "Where will you get the coal?" they asked him. "There is none in the old mines or the railroad yards."

"Yes, that is true," he answered. "But the people of Silverton have coal. I will go to their shops and houses and ask them for it."

And that is what the old man did. Up and down the streets of Silverton he trudged, knocking on doors. People everywhere gave him their precious coal. For they knew that the railroad had to be rebuilt before the winter snows came. Without it their little mountain town would be stranded. People might even starve or freeze to death. And such a terrible thing must not be allowed to happen.

Under the old man's leadership, crews labored furiously to repair the tracks. They worked both down the canyon from Silverton and up the canyon from Durango. From morning till night the clang of their hammers echoed along the river. The old gentleman checked carefully on their

Otto Mears' "Golden Ribbon" Toll Road, built in the early
1880s, later became Colorado's Million Dollar Highway.

progress. Up and down the tracks puffed his little black locomotive. From time to time his silk-hatted head popped out of the window. The sight of the seventy-year-old engineer chugging along the tracks, beard flying, spurred the men on. They worked faster and faster in their race against winter.

At last, after nine long weeks, the final piece of track was spiked into place. How the people cheered as the train from Durango, loaded with food and coal, pulled into Silverton! "Old white-whiskers" was at the throttle. No sooner had he stepped from the train than the skies darkened and snow began falling over the mountains. In a few hours the drifts were piled deep around the houses and stores of Silverton. But the townspeople did not mind. Their bins were full of coal and their stores overflowing with groceries. Thanks to the quick thinking of "old white-whiskers," they had won their race against winter.

Who was this heroic old gentleman who saved the town of Silverton? His name was Otto Mears, and he was one of the most important people in early day Colorado. Mr. Mears was born in 1840 in Russia. His childhood was unhappy. His parents died when he was less than four years old. Before coming to the United States he had lived with his uncles in Russia and England. When he was ten they sent him to stay with relatives in New York.

But life was difficult for a shy boy in a strange, new land. His English was poor and he did not fit in well. So at age fifteen he was sent by ship to still another uncle in San Francisco. Otto did not know that this uncle had already left for Australia. When the boy arrived in California there was no one to meet him. Otto had become a homeless orphan. But some people who ran a rooming house took an interest in him. They helped him find his first job, selling newspapers.

For the next few years, Otto worked hard at many jobs. He clerked, milked cows, and drove a team which hauled freight. He even mined gold for awhile in California and Nevada. But he did not strike it lucky. After the Civil War, Otto came to Colorado. He opened a store in the little town of Conejos (Cone-ay-hos) in the San Luis Valley. There he built the valley's first saw mill. Nails were so expensive in those days that he put it together with rawhide and wooden pegs.

Later he built a gristmill which ground wheat into flour. The wheat, which he raised himself, he sold to the army. But they paid him very little for it. Then suddenly, gold was discovered near Leadville. Wise Otto Mears saw a chance to make his fortune. He would freight his wheat up over Poncha Pass and sell it to the miners! But getting it there, he soon discovered, was not easy. For there was no road over the pass. Otto's horse-drawn wagons lurched along over the rocky ground. It rained and his wheels got stuck in the mud. Then, near the top of the pass, Otto had an accident. One of the wagons tipped over, spilling out most of his valuable grain. This was too much for Otto. He decided right then and there to hack out a toll road over the pass. And he did!

Soon he was building roads all over the mountains. For both gold and silver had been discovered in the San Juans. Miners, hoping to strike it rich, came swarming over the new roads. Later, Mears turned some of them into railroads.

Many of Mears's roads are no longer in use. But one very famous one is. This is the breathtaking Million Dollar Highway which loops over the mountains from Ouray to Silverton. Mears did not name it that. He simply called his early toll road the "Golden Ribbon." It was a dirt road gouged out of solid rock along a thousand-foot-high shelf.

In later years the high, narrow roadway was paved and widened. Some people say that it was named the Million Dollar Highway because it cost more than a million dollars to rebuild it. Others claim that the old, dirt roadbed was full

The Denver and Rio Grande "baby train" chugging along high over Animas Canyon enroute to Silverton. It was said that a winding narrow gauge line could turn a curve on the brim of a Mexican sombrero!

of gold bearing gravel. Regardless of how it got its name, people agree that it is one of the most magnificent highways in Colorado. Along its route, scattered over Red Mountain, lie the ashes of the man who built it. You can see his picture in one of the stained glass windows of our Capitol dome in Denver. Spunky little Otto Mears was truly the "Pathfinder of the San Juans."

* * * *

The Durango-Silverton Railroad, which Mears helped to rebuild, is still running. It is one of the last narrow-gauge railroads in the United States. But it no longer hauls rich ore. Today it carries tourists! Every summer hundreds of passengers board its yellow coaches for the thrilling ride to Silverton. Their hair gets sooty, and black cinders sting their eyes. But nobody seems to mind. People are too busy enjoying the scenery on their forty-five mile trip into yesterday!

La Caverna del Oro (The Cave of Gold)

Do you like stories about pirates and buried treasure?
Of course there were no pirate ships in Colorado! But
hidden in our mountains are secret caves where the early
Spanish explorers, according to legend, buried real gold.
This is a story, which some swear is true, about one of
these caves—known as La Caverna del Oro. This mys-
terious cave is high above timberline, in the Sangre de
Cristo (Blood of Christ) mountains of southern Colorado.
It is only a few miles from the town of Westcliffe.

The cave was first discovered over 100 years ago by a man named Elisha Horn. He was climbing Marble Mountain one day when he stumbled upon a skeleton clad in Spanish armor. An arrow was still sticking out of its bony back! Painted on the gray rocks above the skeleton was a very old, red cross. (You can still see it faintly to this day.) Near the faded cross, he found the entrance to the cave. We don't know if Mr. Horn ever explored it very far. He probably did not because in those days people didn't have flashlights. Anyhow, the cave was scary and dangerous. Wild animals might have been hiding there.

Nothing more was heard about the cave until the 1920s. Then a U.S. forest ranger and some Colorado Mountain Club members explored part of it. An old Mexican woman had told the ranger of Spanish gold buried deep in the earth, behind a set of padlocked wooden doors. The 105-year-old woman remembered that when she was a child, her people tried to explore the cave. They would wrap a blanket around a heavy stone. Then they would throw it down into the hole. But the strong winds in the cave always blew the blanket back to the surface.

Some people in the Colorado Mountain Club went down 500 feet into the cave. But they did not discover any wooden doors or gold. They did find a ladder they believed was about 200 years old, and a hammer that was probably made in the 1600s—over 300 years ago! (The first Spanish explorers came to Colorado in the late 1500s. There were no other white men but Spaniards in the land for most of the 1600s.) Lower down on the mountain, hidden among the aspen trees, the Mountain Club people found the ruins of an old fort. All that was left were several deep holes lined with stone. Had these perhaps been rifle pits? Many arrowheads lay scattered about on the hillsides. The fort (if that's what it was) lay on top of a high hill. So the Spaniards must have had a sweeping view of the valley below. Were they watching for the approach of Indian attackers? We do not know.

But there is more to tell about the cave. Through the years other "spelunkers" (cave hunters) have explored it. At different times, people have uncovered a windlass (rope and bucket for hauling things), a clay jug, and a shovel, among other things. And deep down in the cave, they say, someone once made the scariest discovery of all: a human skeleton chained by the neck to a wall! No gold has ever been found. But the cave has so many rooms, passages, holes and chutes that it will probably never be fully explored. It takes lots of courage to shinny 650 feet down a rope into the slimy, freezing blackness—where there are only bats to keep you company!

So the gold may never be found. But that doesn't mean it isn't there. Some people think that the entrance by the cross is just an escape route. They say that the true entrance lies hidden lower down on the mountainside. One of the arms of the cross is supposed to point to it. This "true" entrance hasn't been discovered either. But perhaps someday it will be. And, according to the legend, whoever finds it will find the gold!

* * * *

The Spaniards were the first white people to explore Colorado. In 1598 they traveled north from Mexico City to make their homes in what is now New Mexico. They brought with them cattle, sheep and goats. They also brought priests who taught the Indians about the Catholic God. The Spanish towns of Santa Fe and Taos were less

than a hundred miles from present Colorado. At that time the southern part of our state also belonged to the king of Spain.

Nobody knows the name of the first Spaniard who set foot in Colorado territory. He could have been a shepherd following his flock of sheep north. Or perhaps he was a prospector searching for gold. The first Spaniards to write about their adventures in Colorado were not exploring. They were chasing runaway Indian slaves who had escaped from northern New Mexico. They chased them far up into what is now eastern Colorado. The Indians were captured and marched back to Taos.

Later, Spaniards sent explorers north to fight the French, who also wanted to own part of Colorado. Other Spaniards crossed our state while trying to find a way west to California. For 250 years the Spaniards wandered in and out of Colorado. Finally, in 1851, they came here to stay. In the lovely San Luis Valley they built San Luis—the first town in Colorado. Today people are still living in our state's oldest town.

We may never find any Spanish gold buried in Colorado. But the Spanish people have given our state something very precious—its name! Colorado is a Spanish word meaning "color red." What looked red to the Spaniards was the water in one of our rivers. The river had this strange color because of the reddish soil in it. It was the Spanish priests who first called it "The Colorado." From this river, more than 100 years later, our state took its name.

Our state was not the only thing that the Spanish named. Many of southern Colorado's towns, counties, mountains and rivers also have Spanish names. The San Juan mountains were named for Catholic "Saint John."

Sangre de Cristo, as you already know, is Spanish for "blood of Christ." The mountains which bear this name have a beautiful, deep red glow at sunrise. Rio is the Spanish word for river. Thus Rio Grande del Norte means "big river of the north." In the Dolores River ("River of Sorrows") a black man once drowned in a flood. Many Spanish words end in vowels. Towns like Pueblo and Alamosa are good examples. Pueblo is Spanish for "town," and Alamosa means "cottonwood." You can find many more Spanish names on a map of Colorado. The Spanish culture has added much to our state.

Colorado Historical Society

Sangre de Cristo mountains in southern Colorado.

Colorado's "Unsinkable" Lady

The night is clear and bitterly cold. There is no moon. Overhead the stars blaze brightly. The sea is as calm and smooth as glass. Eighteen lifeboats bob about gently in the waves. A few hundred yards away, a huge ocean liner is sinking rapidly into the Atlantic. Its lights are still shining. But its big, black smokestacks tilt crazily against the sky. As the bow dips down, the stern rises higher and higher out of the water. Suddenly there is an earsplitting explosion. One of the smokestacks topples over, showering the air with sparks and billowing steam. The ship tilts even more steeply.

As everything movable crashes loose, an unearthly roar thunders across the water. The big ship now rises straight up out of the sea. Hundreds of little ant like figures dangle from the end of it. The people in the lifeboats gasp in horror as the tiny figures drop like flies into the ocean. For a few moments the big ship hangs in the air like an enormous, lighted skyscraper. Its giant propellers gleam in the darkness. Then the lights go out and the huge vessel plunges downward into the sea.

The screaming is terrible as hundreds of people thrash about in the ice cold water. Even the strongest swimmers must die of exposure if they are not soon rescued. But most of the lifeboats are already too far away. Inside boat number six, twenty-eight people—mostly women and children—huddle together in the freezing darkness. Their boat is less than half full. And the frantic calls keep drifting across the water. So the women beg the man who is steering to turn back. But he refuses. "We cannot risk upsetting the boat," he tells them. "We would surely sink if any more people tried to climb aboard."

The ladies strongly disagree. But they do not argue. They do what they can to make the survivors in the boat more comfortable. One well-dressed woman removes an expensive shawl. She places it about the shoulders of a little girl who is crying. Another lady wraps her sable stole (a kind of fur) about the legs of a sooty fireman. She ties the tails about his ankles, as he thanks her through chattering teeth.

Boat 6, with only two men rowing, moves on. It is heading for a far away light on the horizon. But it seems clear after a while that they will never reach it. The man who is steering gives up in despair. "All is lost," he announces to the terrified, half-frozen passengers. "We have no food, no water, no compass and no charts. And we are hundreds of miles from land. We don't even know in which direction we are traveling. There is simply no hope."

The men rowing seem to agree. They drop their oars and sit staring helplessly over the water. At this moment a tall woman, dressed in a black velvet suit, steps forward. She is the same woman who gave her fur stole to the fireman. There is something commanding about her. "Ladies!" she calls out in a loud voice. "Are we going to let these cowardly men give up on us so easily?"

"NO!" scream back the women.

"That's the spirit!" cries their leader. She points to the sky. "We've got the north star above and plenty of muscle power here below. Now grab those oars—this boat is going places!"

But the man in charge does not like what is happening. He moves toward the tall woman. "Stay away from those oars!" he barks. "*I* am in charge of this boat!"

"You are in charge of nothing!" she shouts back. "If you had your way we'd all sit here and freeze to death. You've got all the blankets, and you've even drunk up all the whiskey. Now you come one step closer and I'll throw you overboard!"

The woman seems to mean business. So the man sinks back under his blanket, muttering insults. The ladies pay no attention. They arrange themselves in pairs, one woman holding an oar while her partner does the pulling. The other men soon join in. The little boat glides on through the night.

Margaret Tobin Brown

Suddenly a distant flash appears on the horizon. "That must have been lightning," says one of the women.

"No, it was just a shooting star," argues another passenger.

They row on for awhile in silence. Then they notice a light coming from the same direction. It is followed by another and another. Then row after row of lights appear. "It's a big steamer firing rockets!" yells a man. "Somebody is coming to rescue us!" The other boats have also spotted the ship. Cheers and yells of relief float over the water.

The big ship is still several hours away. But the people in the little boat row faster. Gradually the sky turns pale and the stars begin to fade. A warm, reddish glow lights up the horizon. As it spreads over the sea, floating chunks of ice sparkle like pink and purple jewels. The large vessel appears with the golden dawn. As it steams toward them over the bright, blue water, the exhausted people stop rowing. They hug and kiss one another. Many of them are crying. They have been adrift all night on the freezing ocean. Some are dangerously ill. And all are badly in need of food, warm clothing and medical care. But it looks, at last, as though their lives will be spared.

* * * *

The ocean liner that went down that night was called the *Titanic*. This huge ship was four city blocks long and eleven stories high. It was supposed to be built so well that it was unsinkable. But it struck an iceberg (around midnight) on its very first trip across the ocean. About two and a half hours later it sank. The date was April 15, 1912. Because there were not enough lifeboats, over 1500 people drowned in the sea. Several people even froze to death in the boats. About 700 survivors were picked up next morning by a vessel named the *Carpathia*. It took the people to New York.

The people in Lifeboat 6 owed their lives to the spunky lady who kept them rowing. This was not all that she did. Once the people were safely aboard the *Carpathia*, it took the ship several days to reach New York. During this time she spent hours nursing the sick and comforting the dying. She got a doctor for a rich, young lady named Mrs. Astor, who was expecting a baby. She also helped many poor, foreign women who were on board. These women, who had lost their husbands and brothers in the sea, could not even speak English. She realized that without friends or money they would surely starve to death in a strange, new land. So she raised $7,000 to help them. Even after the *Carpathia* docked in New York, she refused to leave it. She had many messages to pass on to the relatives of people who had died on the ship.

Who was this heroic lady who did so much for so many? Her name was Molly Brown—and she came from Colorado. She had once been married to Jim ("J.J.") Brown, part owner of Leadville's rich Little Jonny mine. Four lions, carved out of stone, decorated the front wall of her fancy mansion in Denver. Her mining money allowed Mrs. Brown to travel all over the world. Some of the wealthiest people in New York and Europe were her friends. But because she had begun life poor and uneducated, she was snubbed by the "important" people of Denver. For many years they laughed at her manners and made fun of the way she talked.

But the sinking of the *Titanic* changed all that. Molly, who became known as "The Unsinkable Mrs. Brown," was suddenly invited everywhere. And people no longer stayed away from the balls and garden parties she gave at her "House of the Lions." Today this famous Denver house is open for tours. Only two sitting lions remain out front. They seem to stand for the courage and unselfishness of Colorado's unsinkable lady.

Western History Department, Denver Public Library

The "House of the Lions"

Graveyard
of the Monsters

On the Colorado-Utah border is one of the strangest graveyards in the world. It is millions of years old. But no people are buried in it—only dinosaurs! How did they get there? Scientists think that long ago a shallow river flowed through this graveyard. Sometimes the river rose quite high and flooded. Dead dinosaurs from miles around were swept along in the swirling current. When the water level dropped again, their bodies came to rest in the sand.

More sand piled on top of them—thousands of feet of sand. Gradually this sand hardened into rock. Then the land began rising slowly. Wind and running water cut down through the rocky layers. It took millions of years for the wind and water to wear away the rock. But at last the sandbar cemetery was uncovered. The bodies of the dinosaurs had all rotted away. Only their bones were left. After being buried for more than 140 million years, they had turned to stone.

Today you can see these petrified dinosaur bones. They lie in one corner of a huge park called Dinosaur National Monument. This park, which is in both Colorado and Utah, covers many miles. It has wild animals, colorful canyons and swiftly flowing rivers. But the dinosaur quarry is the most unusual part of it. Here a museum has been built right into the side of a rocky cliff.

This cliff was once the sandbar cemetery. Hundreds of bones lie jumbled about in it. They look like the messy remains of some giant's turkey dinner! You can watch workmen picking at the rock around them with hammers and chisels. The men are not trying to dig the bones out. They are simply cutting away the rock so that you can see them better. After being shellacked, most of the ancient fossils are left in place. You can see them just as they were buried, millions of years ago.

What was Colorado like during the days of the dinosaurs? You may have read or been told that it was a great, swampy area. But scientists no longer believe this. They have been studying the rocks at the quarry. And they have decided that Colorado's dinosaurs lived in a somewhat dry, sunny climate. The amount of rainfall was prob-

Dinosaurs once roamed freely where the Yampa River joins the meandering Green at Steamboat Rock, in colorful Dinosaur National Monument.

ably about the same as it is today. Shrubs and evergreen trees dotted the barren landscape. But there were few large rivers or lakes. And of course there were no Rocky Mountains.

The dinosaurs on these dry plains lived much like animals in East Africa do today. Like zebras and antelopes they traveled in herds. Some of them could run fairly fast. The huge plant eaters used their long, giraffe-like necks for reaching into trees. Some of them could reach the topmost branches by rearing up on their powerful hind legs and tails. They ate cones and prickly evergreen needles. And the smaller meat eating dinosaurs ate *them*! (Because of their tremendous size, the meat eaters probably attacked them in packs.)

What kind of dinosaurs roamed through Colorado 140 million years ago? The bones of both meat eaters and

Skeleton of Diplodocus, longest of the dinosaurs.

plant eaters have been found at the quarry. (A few baby dinosaurs have even been unearthed.) The first dinosaur ever discovered there was a *Brontosaurus*. A scientist named Earl Douglas spotted him in 1909. Eight of his tailbones were sticking out of the rock. The skeleton of this long-necked plant eater ended up in a museum in Pittsburgh, Pennsylvania. But another skeleton taken from the quarry found a home in Denver. This was *Diplodocus*, longest of the dinosaurs. You can see all 75½ feet of him at the Denver Museum of Natural History. He, too, was a plant eater.

The quarry's most common dinosaur is *Stegosaurus*. A big model of him stands outside the entrance to the Dinosaur National Monument museum. This strange looking plant eater had a double row of plates down his back. He must have looked something like a walking artichoke plant. But one slap of his heavy, spiked tail sent enemies flying.

Camarasaurus, a medium-sized plant eater, left one of the most interesting bones at the quarry. A very rude dinosaur must have stepped on him once. For two of his badly smashed tailbones have been found fused together.

Most of the quarry dinosaurs were peaceful plant eaters. But the remains of a fierce killer dinosaur have also been uncovered. This was flesh eating *Allosaurus*. He walked on his hind legs and had vicious teeth and claws. We can't prove, of course, that he actually attacked bigger dinosaurs. He may have just feasted off their dead bodies at the cemetery. Whether *Allosaurus* gulped his food down dead or alive, we know for certain that this ferocious fellow didn't go hungry!

The quarry dinosaurs all lived in Colorado at about the same time. You are probably wondering if *Tyrannosaurus*

Rex was here also. He was! But he didn't come along until millions of years later. The teeth of the "tyrant lizard" have turned up around Denver. Remains of his favorite meal, the duck-billed *Trachodon*, have been found nearby. And many a tough *Triceratops* charged across the plains of Colorado. Mr. "three-horn-face" must have looked something like an army tank mounted with machine guns. He was not the easiest meal for *Tyrannosaurus* to sink his teeth into!

For millions of years these monsters ruled the land that would one day become Colorado. Why did they finally die out? The scientists really do not know. Some think that the tremendous heat rays given off by an exploding star may have killed the dinosaurs. Others feel that changes in weather and climate probably wiped them out. As the earth grew colder, plant life certainly changed. The dinosaurs may have slowly starved to death. Or perhaps some terrible disease finished them.

The riddle of the disappearing dinosaurs may never be solved. But dinosaur detectives keep working on it. And do you know what some of them have recently decided? That the dinosaurs, like you and me, were warm-blooded animals! Perhaps their very name, which means "terrible lizard," will have to be changed. For in many ways, they were not like reptiles at all. And the scientists have made an even more amazing discovery. Some of the small, meat eating dinosaurs had bones almost exactly like those of the first bird, *Archaeopteryx* (Ar-kee-op-ter-iks). A few of them may even have had feathers. So perhaps the dinosaurs are not extinct after all. They have just changed their form. Dozens of them invade our backyards daily— in the lovely shape of birds!

Ouray Meets "Big Chief Hot Stuff"

Ouray, the great chief of the Ute Indians, took down his rifle and carefully inspected it. Yes, he would be ready for tomorrow's visitor. One of the chief's spies had warned him that a young warrior nicknamed "Hot Stuff" was coming to kill him. This did not surprise Ouray. He knew that many lesser chiefs hated him because he had refused to fight the white man. It did not matter to Ouray that they thought him a coward.

How stupid these young warriors were not to see the importance of keeping friends with the powerful whites! True, the white men had lied to the Indians and broken their promises. But what could the Utes hope to gain by fighting? There were many more white people than Indians and they had more guns. If they made war, many Utes would be killed, and the rest driven even further from their shining mountains.

No—the gold-crazy white men were here to stay. The Indian would just have to make the best of it. Ouray smiled to himself as he cleaned and loaded his rifle. He had heard about this Hot Stuff and how he got his strange name. He had been sent to an Indian school in the east, where he studied chemistry. But he was very careless and sloppy. One day in class some chemicals he was using in an experiment exploded. "Hot Stuff," as he was nicknamed, landed in the hospital. Now the hot-headed young man was back on the Indian reservation in Colorado. He planned to murder Ouray, take his place as chief, and make war on the whites!

"Are we going to move camp before sunup tomorrow?" Ouray's wife, Chipeta, asked her husband.

"No," he replied, "we'll stay here and wait for Hot Stuff."

"What will you do when he comes?" she asked, half fearing his answer.

"Kill him, of course," said Ouray calmly.

"But . . ."

"He will make trouble for our people if he lives," explained the chief. "He would turn the whites into our

Chief Ouray and Chipeta about 1885

enemies. They must continue to be our friends. Do not worry, Chipeta. I will do what is best for the Blue Sky People."

The next morning Chipeta was very nervous. Somewhere out in the sagebrush, high above Leopard Creek, Hot Stuff must be skulking along the ridge. He might be watching them right now! The minutes dragged by. Morning became afternoon, and Chipeta breathed a little easier. Maybe he wasn't coming after all. Perhaps the hot-blooded young buck had thought it over and changed his mind.

Chipeta slipped out to look around. Her gaze traveled slowly along the horizon. Suddenly, she ran inside. "He's up on the slope back of us hiding in the brush," she told her husband breathlessly. "His calico horse is tied to the big fir."

Painting of the tragic Meeker Massacre of 1879 which caused most of the Ute Indians to be driven out of Colorado on to reservations.

Ouray's lips tightened. He did not enjoy killing. But this dangerous enemy of peace must be gunned down like a mad coyote. Grabbing his rifle, he hurried outside. He aimed it up toward the slope, in Hot Stuff's direction. Seconds passed . . . he stood motionless, his finger frozen on the trigger. Then a brown blur streaked from behind a bush. The crack of Ouray's rifle shattered the stillness. Hot Stuff tumbled over into the brush. Then he lay still. He would no longer beat the war drums and boast of becoming chief—his neck was broken. Ouray, the white man's friend, was still in command of the Utes.

* * * *

"Hot Stuff" was not the only Indian who plotted to murder Ouray. The great chief had to kill four other Utes who wanted to make war on the whites. Because he controlled his unhappy people so well, there were few Ute outbreaks during the 1870s. But Chief Ouray had a hard time. During these years, gold was discovered in the San Juan mountains. The Utes were forced to sign treaties giving away much of their mountain land.

Unfortunately, Ouray could do nothing to stop an Indian massacre which took place at Meeker, one day in 1879. The trouble began when a man named Nathan Meeker tried to make the northern Utes learn farming. The freedom loving Indians hated the white man's plows and barbed wire fences. So when Meeker plowed up their horse racing track, they made war. Meeker and several other white men were killed. After this fight, most of the Utes were ordered out of Colorado and onto reservations in Utah. A few were allowed to keep a small southwestern corner of the state. And that is where the Ute reservation remains today.

Throughout all these troubles Chief Ouray remained friendly to the white man to whom he always kept his word. This remarkable Indian spoke four languages: Spanish, English, Ute and Apache. He was probably smarter than most of the whites with whom he made treaties. Ouray once said: "The agreement an Indian makes to a United States treaty is like the agreement a buffalo makes with the hunter when pierced with arrows. All he can do is lie down and give in."

Ouray is pictured in one of the stained glass windows in our state capitol dome at Denver. Also, a town, a county, and a mountain are named for him. Ouray means "arrow," and Chipeta is the Ute word for "white singing bird." You can see the great chief's things, and those of his wife, at the Ute Indian Museum near Montrose. Chipeta is buried nearby. Ouray's remains rest on the Colorado Ute Reservation. Happily, he did not live long enough to see his people driven from their shining mountains.

Colorado's Gifts to the Nation

Perhaps you have read about or seen pictures of two famous national monuments, the Lincoln Memorial and the Tomb of the Unknown Soldier. If you've been to Washington, D.C., our nation's capital, you may have even visited them. Each year more than two million people do. They come from all over the world. Every day hundreds watch the changing of the guard at the Tomb of the Unknown Soldier. People also enjoy standing before the huge Lincoln Memorial at night, when the statue of Lincoln is softly lighted. Few tourists realize, however, that most of the marble used in building these two monuments came from Colorado!

On the western slope of the Rockies, not far from Glenwood Springs, there is a tiny ghost town called Marble. High above it is Treasure Mountain Dome—a peak made up almost entirely of this rare, beautiful stone. Some of the marble found here is among the purest and whitest in the world. The mountain also has green, pink, blue and black marble.

How did it get there? The story of the marble's formation sounds like magic. Over 300 million years ago there were no Rocky Mountains. Central Colorado was a flat land, covered by a shallow sea. Billions of fish and tiny animals with shells lived in the warm, salty water. When they died their bodies sank to the bottom. The soft parts rotted away, but the harder bones and shells were pressed into the mud. (Much as you'd press your finger into a piece of clay.) As more and more mud was laid over them, the shells pressed tightly together.

Then the first mountains were lifted up out of the sea. The black mud mixed with shells dried up. Later it hardened into a kind of rock we call limestone. The animal shapes still pressed into it became fossils. As the land rose higher, streams began to run through it, washing away the limestone. The land was not rising as fast as it was being washed away. So in time these first mountains, which were called the Ancestral Rockies, disappeared. Limestone pebbles found at the bottom of today's mountains are all that is left of them. (Everybody has ancestors. They are people in your family who were born before you, but are no longer living. Can you figure out why these early mountains were called "ancestral"?)

For the next 165 million years the limestone, once again, lay buried under a shallow sea. Dinosaurs with horns and armor now roamed the land. Then about 65 million years ago, the real Rockies were born. Masses of hot, flowing rock called "magma" rose up from deep inside the earth. The fiery magma destroyed all the fossil remains in the limestone. The crystals now grew larger and actually changed their shape. The black limestone, buried deep in the earth, was slowly turning into sparkling, white marble.

But a few more million years were to pass before man would find it. The first marble was not taken out of the quarries until the late 1800s. (A quarry is a large open hole where stone is cut, dug, or blasted out of the earth.) One of the earliest buildings partly constructed of it was our Colorado State Capitol, built in the 1890s. Builders knew that marble was a perfect stone to use. It doesn't chip, burn or wear away. And neither heat, cold, nor moisture seem to affect it. (It does have one enemy: air pollution. Marble buildings in big cities sometimes get so

National Park Service

The thirty-six columns which hold up the Lincoln
Memorial were carved from Colorado marble.

dirty that they almost look black. Special chemicals are
used to clean them.)

Now, how did Colorado's marble get to the nation's
capital? In 1911, the United States government decided to
build a memorial to President Abraham Lincoln. They
held a sort of contest about where they should buy the
marble to construct it. Marble samples were sent to
Washington, D. C. from all over the world. Colorado's
snow white marble was judged to be the purest and most
beautiful. It was also the hardest. So in 1914, the
Colorado-Yule Marble Company won the contract for the
outside of the famous building. (The giant statue of Lincoln, which sits inside, was carved out of Georgia marble.
It is 19 feet high.)

Entrance to one of the abandoned marble quarries above the ghost town of Marble. Ahead of the boy is a deep dropoff.

Work on the Memorial soon began. A new shop with special equipment was set up at the marble mill. Thirty-six columns, each forty-six feet high and seven feet around, had to be built. These would hold up the building. Each three-story-high column would stand for one of the states in the Union when Lincoln was president. It would have been impossible to quarry whole columns out of the mountain. Eighteen hundred small blocks of stone had to be cut. "Fluting" machines then carved round curves on each block. Finally, 600 freight cars carried the finished pieces to the nation's capital. Here they were fitted together to make the columns. (Much as you'd build with blocks.) The huge monument was completed in 1922.

But Colorado was still to produce the largest *single* piece of marble ever quarried in the world. This was used in the Tomb of the Unknown Soldier, at Arlington National Cemetery. In this tomb lies the body of a soldier killed in France during World War I. Fifty thousand U.S. soldiers were killed in battle during that war. It was impossible to identify all their bodies. So one nameless soldier was chosen to be buried in the tomb, in honor of them all. On the marble slab are carved these words: "HERE RESTS IN HONORED GLORY AN AMERICAN SOLDIER KNOWN BUT TO GOD." Sentries guard it day and night (Two more unknown soldiers rest nearby. One fought in World War II and the other in the Korean War.)

Colorado's quarry was the only one in the world large enough to produce the huge block needed for the tomb. Seventy-five men worked for more than a year to cut it out of the mountain. At first the uncut block weighed 124 tons. (That's more than the weight of ninety Volkswagens!) While it was still on the floor of the quarry they trimmed it down with a wire saw to fifty-six tons. It was now 14½ feet long and stood 7½ feet high.

A special machine from Vermont was sent to lift it out of the quarry. Everyone held their breath on that January day as the huge crane leaned out over the opening. Slowly it lowered its thick, wire cable into the depths below. When it was 125 feet down, the block was attached to the cable. But before they could lift it out, the workers had to test the strength of the ropes. So for about fifteen minutes it just hung there in the air. Then inch by inch they began painstakingly hoisting upward. As they did so, a three foot hunk of steel under the hoist broke into pieces. One of these hit a man over the heart, knocking him out for twenty minutes. Luckily, he recovered. (The men at the quarry did difficult and dangerous work. Every winter, in twenty-below-zero temperatures, they had to clear the railroad tracks of snowdrifts and avalanches. Sometimes they even had to dig their way through ice tunnels to get to their houses. In summer there were floods and runaway trolley wrecks.)

At last the mammoth stone reached the top of the quarry. A special railroad track had been built to bring it down the mountain. Now it was on its way to the mill. At the bottom of the slope it was moved to the electric trolley track. They had to make sure that it wouldn't speed out of control on the steep grade. So they skidded it down on a homemade railroad car without rear wheels. They moved so slowly that one of the locomotives pulling the car actually burned out its brakes. It took them four days to travel about four miles to the mill! People took pictures all along the way.

Just before they got to the mill they had to cross the Crystal River. The men were afraid the bridge might collapse under the heavy load. So they disconnected the two locomotives. Then they had the block moved across by itself on a special flatcar. Upon arriving at the mill yard, the marble slab was closely guarded for several days and nights. (This was to keep souvenir hunters from chipping off small pieces.) Then it began its long railroad journey east. First it was shipped to Vermont for finishing. Finally, on November 11, 1932, it was placed at the entrance to Arlington National Cemetery. And there it stands today. The Tomb and the Lincoln Memorial are Colorado's two great gifts to the nation.

* * * *

Marble is no longer being taken out of the quarries. The old mill buildings by the Crystal River are gone. But the huge chunks of marble that were part of their foundation are still there. They look like pieces of an old, deserted temple lying among the weeds. The electric trolley tracks that once went up the mountain are also gone. In their place is a winding dirt road. You can hike right up to the old quarries and look down into their icy depths. But you'd better be careful. There is nothing to stop you from going over the edge!

United States Army

Sentry guards the Tomb of the Unknown Soldier, at Arlington National Cemetery just across the Potomac River from the nation's capital.

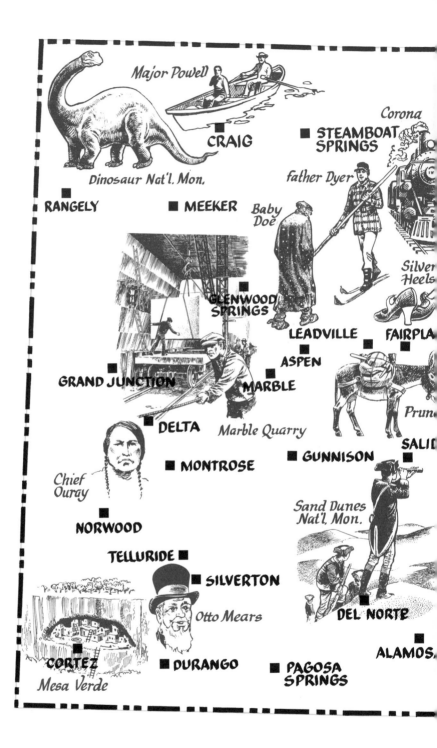

Major Powell

CRAIG

STEAMBOAT SPRINGS

Corona

Dinosaur Nat'l. Mon.

father Dyer

RANGELY

MEEKER

Baby Doe

GLENWOOD SPRINGS

Silver Heels

LEADVILLE

FAIRPLA

GRAND JUNCTION

ASPEN

MARBLE

DELTA

Marble Quarry

SALI

Chief Ouray

MONTROSE

GUNNISON

Sand Dunes Nat'l. Mon.

Prun

NORWOOD

TELLURIDE

SILVERTON

Otto Mears

DEL NORTE

CORTEZ

DURANGO

PAGOSA SPRINGS

ALAMOS

Mesa Verde

Isabella Bird

■ FT. COLLINS

STERLING
■

■ GREELEY

■ FT MORGAN

Molly Brown

■ BOULDER

DENVER
■

Kit Carson

■DEN

■ LIMON

■ COLORADO SPRINGS
Pike's Peak

Cattle Drives

■ PUEBLO

Bent's Fort

■ LAMAR

■ANON ITY

LA JUNTA

■ WALSENBURG   *"Uncle Dick" Wootton*

ve of Gold   ■ TRINIDAD

BIBLIOGRAPHY

Arps, Louisa and Kingery, Elinor Eppich. *High Country Names*. Boulder, Colorado: Rocky Mountain Nature Association, 1972.

Bakker, Robert T. *A New Image For Dinosaurs*. In Science Year—The World Book Science Annual—1977. Chicago: Field Enterprises Educational Corporation, 1976 (p. 50-64).

Bancroft, Caroline. *Colorful Colorado*. Boulder, Colorado: Johnson Publishing Co., 1959.

Bancroft, Caroline. *Two Burros of Fairplay*. Boulder, Colorado: Johnson Publishing Co., 1968.

Bancroft, Caroline. *Unique Ghost Towns and Mountain Spots*. Boulder, Colorado: Johnson Publishing Co., 1967.

Bancroft, Caroline. *The Unsinkable Mrs. Brown*. Boulder, Colorado: Johnson Publishing Co., 1963.

Bartlett, Richard A. *Great Surveys of the American West*. Norman: University of Oklahoma Press, 1962.

Bean, Luther. *Once Upon A Time*. Alamosa, Colorado: Ye Olde Print Shoppe, 1975.

Bean, Luther. *Land of the Blue Sky People*. Alamosa, Colorado: Ye Olde Print Shoppe, 1975.

Beebe, Lucius and Clegg, Charles. *Narrow Gauge in the Rockies*. Berkeley, California: Howell-North Press, 1958.

Bird, Isabella. *A Lady's Life in the Rocky Mountains*. University of Oklahoma Press, 1960. (Reprinted by Ballantine Books, Inc., New York, 1971.)

Bollinger, Edward T., and Bauer, Frederick. *The Moffat Road*. Chicago: Sage Books, The Swallow Press Inc., 1962.

Bollinger, Edward T. *Rails That Climb*. 2nd Ed. Santa Fe: The Rydal Press, 1950 (Chapter 9, "Nine Extras East, Light," pp. 103-117).

Bueler, Gladys R. *Colorado's Colorful Characters*. Boulder, Colorado: Smoking Stack Press, 1975.

Campion, Nardi Reeder. *Kit Carson, Pathfinder of the West* In Adventures In Buckskin. Edited with commentary by Bennett Wayne. Champaign, Illinois: Garrard Publishing Co., 1973.

Carhart, Arthur H., *Colorado*. New York: Coward-McCann, Inc., 1932.

Conard, Howard Louis. *Uncle Dick Wootton, The Pioneer Frontiersman of the Rocky Mountain Region*. Edited by Milo Milton Quaife. Chicago: The Lakeside Press, 1957.

Coquoz, Rene L. *The Saga of H.A.W. Tabor*. Boulder, Colorado: Johnson Publishing Co., 1968.

Davidson, Levette J. and Blake, Forrester, Editors, *Rocky Mountain Tales*. University of Oklahoma Press, 1947. (Reprinted in New York: Ballantine Books, 1971.)

Davidson, Levette Jay, and Bostwick, Prudence. *The Literature of the Rocky Mountain West, 1803-1903*. Caldwell, Idaho: The Caxton Printers, Ltd., 1939.

Dobie, J. Frank. *The Longhorns*. Boston: Little Brown and Co., 1941.

Downey, Matthew T. and Metcalf, Fay D. *Colorado, Crossroads of the West*. Boulder, Colorado: Pruett Publishing Co., 1976.

Dyer, John L. *The Snowshoe Itinerant*. Cincinnati: Published for the author by Cranston and Stowe, 1889. (Reprinted by the Father Dyer United Methodist Church, 1975.)

Eberhart, Perry. *Treasure Tales of the Rockies*. Denver: Sage Books, Alan Swallow, Publisher, 1961.

Ellis, Amanda. *Legends and Tales of the Rockies*. Denton Printing Co., 1954.

Emrich, Duncan. *It's An Old Wild West Custom*. New York: The Vanguard Press, Inc., 1949.

Federal Writer's Program of the Works Projects Administration of the State of Colorado. *Colorado, A Guide to the Highest State*. American Guide Series. New York: Hastings House, 1941.

Ferrell, Mallory Hope. *Silver San Juan—The Rio Grande Southern*. Boulder, Colorado: Pruett Publishing Co., 1973.

Frandsen, Maude Linstrom. *Our Colorado*. Rev. ed. Denver: The Old West Publishing Co., 1959, 1964, 1966.

Good, John M., White, Theodore E., and Stucker, Gilbert F. *The Dinosaur Quarry*. National Park Services (Government Document), Washington, D.C., 1958.

Gray, Arthur Amos. *Men Who Built the West*. Caldwell, Idaho: The Caxton Printers Ltd., 1945.

Hafen, Ann and Hafen, LeRoy R. *Our State: Colorado*. Denver: The Old West Publishing Co., 1971.

Hagood, Allen, *Dinosaur, the Story Behind the Scenery*. Las Vegas, Nevada: K.C. Publications, 1972.

Jefferson, James, Delaney, Robert A. and Thompson, Gregory C. *The Southern Utes, A Tribal History*. Ignacio, Colorado: Southern Ute Tribe, 1972.

Jocknick, Sidney. *Early Days on the Western Slope of Colorado and Campfire Chats with Otto Mears, the Pathfinder, from 1871 to 1883*. Rio Grande, 1968.

Lavender, David. *Bent's Fort*. Lincoln: University of Nebraska Press, 1954. (First Bison Book printing, March, 1972.)

Lee, W. Storrs. *Colorado, A Literary Chronicle*. New York: Funk and Wagnalls, 1970.

Lord, Walter. *A Night to Remember*. New York: Holt, 1976.

McCoy, Dell and Collman, Russ. *The Crystal River Pictorial*. Denver: Sundance Limited, 1972.

McNitt, Frank. *Richard Wetherill: Anasazi*. Rev. ed. Albuquerque: The University of New Mexico Press, 1966.

Moody, Ralph. *Kit Carson and the Wild Frontier*. New York: Landmark Books, Random House, Inc., 1955.

Nesbit, Paul W. *Long's Peak, Its Story and a Climbing Guide*. Rev. Boulder, Colorado: Norman L. Nesbit, 1972.

O'Brien, Theresa. *The Bitter Days of Baby Doe Tabor and Memories of the High Country*, 1963.

Pearl, Richard M. *Landforms of Colorado*. Colorado Springs: Earth Science Publishing Co., 1975.

Tales, Trails and Tommyknockers

Powell, John Wesley. *The Exploration of the Colorado River and It's Canyons*. New York: Dover Publications Inc., 1961. (Originally Flood and Vincent, 1895.)

Richmond, Gerald M. *Raising the Roof of the Rockies*. Rocky Mountain Nature Association, Inc., National Park Service, U.S. Department of the Interior, 1974.

Rickard, Kent. *Highlights of Colorado History for Non-historians*. Littleton, Colorado: 1974.

Rockwell, Wilson. *The Utes: A Forgotten People*. Sage Books, 1956.

Sumner, David. *Colorado/Southwest*. Denver: Sanborn Souvenir Company, Inc., 1973.

Trimble, Stephen A. *Great Sand Dunes*. Globe, Arizona: Southwest Parks and Monuments Association, Paragon Press.

Ullman, James Ramsey. *Down the Colorado with Major Powell*. Cambridge, Massachusetts: North Star Books-The Riverside Press, 1960.

Urquhart, Lena M. *Colorow, The Angry Chieftain*. Denver: Golden Bell Press, 1968.

Vandenbusche, Duane and Myers, Rex. *Marble Colorado, City of Stone*. Denver: Golden Bell Press, 1970.

Vestal, Stanley, *Kit Carson*. Boston and New York: Houghton Mifflin Co., 1928.

Vestal, Stanley. *Mountain Men*. Boston: Houghton Mifflin Co., 1937.

Wibberley, Leonard. *Wes Powell, Conqueror of the Grand Canyon*. New York: Ariel Books, Farrar, Straus and Cudahy, American Book-Stratford Press, Inc., 1958.

Wolle, Muriel Sibell. *Stampede to Timberline*. Third Printing. Boulder: Published by Muriel Sibell Wolle, 1949.